The Charisma Factor

How To Develop Your Natural Leadership Ability

Robert J. Richardson, Ph.D.
S. Katharine Thayer

PRENTICE HALL
Englewood Cliffs, New Jersey 07632

Prentice-Hall International, Inc., *London*
Prentice-Hall of Australia, Pty. Ltd., *Sydney*
Prentice-Hall of Canada, Inc., *Toronto*
Prentice-Hall Hispanoamericana, S.A., *Mexico*
Prentice-Hall of India Private Ltd., *New Dehli*
Prentice-Hall of Japan, Inc. *Tokyo*
Prentice-Hall of Southeast Asia Pte., Ltd., *Singapore*
Editora Prentice-Hall do Brasil Ltda., *Rio de Janeiro*

10 9 8 7 6 5 4 3 2 1

Library of Congress Cataloging-in-Publication Data

Richardson, Robert J.
  The charisma factor : how to develop your natural leadership
ability / by Robert J. Richardson & S. Katharine Thayer.
    p. cm.

  Includes bibliograhpica.l references and index.
  ISBN 0-13-904368-3
  1. Leadership. 2. Charisma (Personality trait) 3. Executive ability.
I. Thayer, S. Katharine. II. Title.
HD57.7.R52   1993
658.4'092—dc20   92-33927
                                                            CIP

ISBN 0-13-904368-3

PRENTICE HALL
Professional Publishing
Englewood Cliffs, NJ 07632
Simon & Schuster. A Paramount Communications Company

PRINTED IN THE UNITED STATES OF AMERICA

Introduction

If there is one challenge that thousands of companies, organizations, political campaigns, and social causes often seem
to share it is the consistent stimulation of excitement, enthusiasm, and dedication in those whose responsibility it is to
get the job done. Far too often work forces stagnate, clients
waver, and supporters become apathetic despite the continuous and aggressive efforts of those in leadership positions.
Regardless of the incentives and motivational techniques
employed, the art of generating personal commitment in
others has seemed to be, at best, a nebulous process. The
exception, of course, has been a certain kind of leader, one
who possesses what we have come to call charisma. Charismatic leaders seem almost magically to draw people in and
create hard-driving teams that are focused, dedicated, and
anxious to commit to their absolute best.

The Charisma Factor is a book for serious leaders seeking
to position themselves and their companies for the 1990s. It
is for those who need to do far more than just influence and
persuade. This unique book is the blueprint of how the great
charismatic leaders have sparked extraordinary followings
and engendered amazing allegiance from others. It is the
step-by-step distinctive process you can follow to ignite the
desire in people to want to follow your leadership and to
enthusiastically perform. It is a strategy that will make an
astounding difference on the level of impact you can have on
others.

The project began when a political consultant posed a simple question to me, "Do you think you could define the personality characteristics of great charismatic leaders?" Instantly my mind began churning with ideas and the ramifications of such a discovery. Just think of it, if organizations could somehow identify this personality trait called charisma in current employees and future job applicants, they would know whom to groom for leadership and how to better measure manpower potential. They could have far greater insights into the very essence of powerful leadership! Because the trait of charisma, whatever it really is, allows one to have a profound impact on others, identifying and cultivating charismatic leaders could exponentially increase the level of performance in company employees. Could it be that some have it and don't know it? Could we really recognize charismatic leaders and train these people to become superstars?

The thought of such incredible possibilities spurred me on to the most focused and dedicated effort of my life. I immersed myself in an academic search for the elusive combination of the personality characteristics that make a person charismatic. I had always believed, as have most other people, that this trait we called charisma was just something you were either born with or not. Either you had it or you didn't. With such a presupposition I naturally aimed my research toward the "fact" that charisma is the result of a specific set of personal qualities. Yet, in the midst of walking down this path with some of the world's charismatic legends I came to an unexpected fork in the road. If charisma was a function of personality, why was it that every great charismatic leader was different from every other? Think about it: John F. Kennedy and Winston Churchill, Ronald Reagan and Dr. Martin Luther King, Jr., even Jesse Jackson and Oliver North, all individuals who were or are extremely charismatic, each having a stunning impact and influence on those around him. Yet each personality is very different. No two are alike.

I was therefore compelled to head down a new, less traveled path and what awaited me at the end was truly an astonishing discovery. Charisma, probably the most powerful of leadership tools, is not at all a function of personality but a very specific form of communication. In fact, every great charismatic leader I studied, from Ronald Reagan back to those in the times of the ancient Greeks, used precisely the same techniques sequenced in exactly the same order. It was not so much that these individuals were "special," but that they intuitively knew how to do something that others did not.

Think for a moment about a powerful charismatic leader you have seen or heard. Whether it was a political figure, a business leader, or a motivational speaker who really touched you, what was it that made this person so distinctive? What was it that made him or her stand so far out in front of the crowd? Was it the person's appearance, the sound of the voice, the way the person moved? Though possibly those factors played a part, the real essence of charisma, that which makes charismatic leaders so distinctive, is the way they make others *feel*. Charisma is the ability to touch the hearts as well as the minds of people. Charismatic leaders know how to make us feel confident, full of pride and enthusiasm, or they can engender just about any other emotion they desire. In fact, if there is anything that charismatic leaders provide that others don't, it is the commodity of emotions.

No wonder charismatic leaders have such a powerful impact. Human beings are emotionally driven creatures. Our everyday performance, abilities, and reactions to life all revolve around how we are feeling at the time. The power of emotions is one of the most basic building blocks of effective leadership, yet it is often overlooked. Even though our culture places more importance on logic than emotions, we are biologically tied to a simple truth: that the emotional state of mind we are in at any given moment will do more to direct our actions than will any other factor.

Every one of us experience days when we are in the mood to go to work and days when we aren't. There are times when, simply because we don't *feel* like being there, even the most basic tasks at work seem unending. Yet, on other days when enthusiasm and accomplishment reign, the time seems

Introduction

magically to disappear. When we are in the appropriate
emotional state of mind, our performance level soars. When
we are not, it plummets. Jack Welch, the president of General
Electric, probably stated it best: "Businesses are powered by
emotions and feelings as much as by money, knowledge,
logic, and technology." This new theme is thrusting companies far ahead of their competition, and charisma, the knowledge and ability to infuse the best in people, is at the core of
their success.

We human beings possess far more energy and ability
than we realize. There is a vast reserve of human talent that
goes virtually untapped in each of us. Access to these reserves are cut off by negative emotions: feelings of laziness,
fear, disinterest, and inferiority. We might dream of great
accomplishments, but we are pulled back into mediocrity
because of an inability to exercise the necessary positive
emotional state needed to accomplish the task.

Yet the distance between status quo and stellar performance is far less than one might believe. The craft of helping
others access their own personal excellence is the quality we
call charisma. Charismatic leaders are able to generate incredible efforts from a work force, steadfast support from
followers, and long-term loyalty from clients. This does not
happen simply because of their genius for organization,
political position, or quality of product but because of the
way they are able to make people feel. By consistently touching others at an emotional level and constantly instilling in
others powerful, uplifting feelings, they are able to assist
others in achieving their absolute best. Their followers naturally then become dedicated supporters, the kind needed to
make great things happen.

Charisma is best thought of as *charismatic communication*. It is a process rather than a trait, combining both verbal
and nonverbal techniques in order to evoke the kinds of
emotions that will inspire action in others. Once the essence
of charismatic communication was defined, I found it was a
fairly simple task to identify the exact verbal and nonverbal
techniques that these charismatic legends used. These tech-

niques are called Emotional Management. Yet, even though I could trace their use to every great charismatic leader, I noticed that other noncharismatic leaders would fall flat on their faces if they used them. For example, Ronald Reagan's speeches were full of verbal Emotional Management techniques. He could inspire millions with what seemed to be simple words. George Bush using the same speech writers and the same verbal Emotional Management techniques, however, could leave the nation unmoved by his words. Though I knew I was on the right track, it was now obvious that there was more to the puzzle.

It was not until I came upon the brilliant work of cultural anthropologist Edward T. Hall that the puzzle became complete. In his research of various cultures he discovered the secret of the unconscious bond that holds both societies and individuals together. This aspect of human interaction is so deeply embedded into the human psyche that few of us are even aware of its existence, let alone have the ability to define it. This is the bond that many have thought of as the "magnetic personality." What this left me with was a blueprint for charismatic leadership. It is the *process* for inspiring and energizing people toward their absolute best; the mechanism for generating a dedicated following. It is the step-by-step methodology history's most powerful and popular leaders used to change the face of their companies, countries, and even the world. Even more exciting, the sequence of techniques that make up Charismatic Communication are the same ones used to create some of the country's most dynamic companies such as Apple, Norwegian Cruise Lines, Disney, and Ben & Jerry's. So versatile is this process that we have successfully used it in diverse situations, from direct political action campaigns to the lecturing of U.S. counterintelligence agents.

Whether you have a leadership position in a major corporation, hold political office, coordinate the efforts of volunteers, or make a living as a sales professional, I trust the information contained in this book will have the remarkable level of impact on your life as it has for so many others.

Robert J. Richardson

Acknowledgments

The writing of a book, as with any other project, is seldom accomplished alone. *The Charisma Factor* is no exception. And for that reason it is only appropriate to mention some of those who made substantial contributions yet did not find their name on the front cover.

The first to come to mind is Neal Moquin, who deserves a very special thank you for his extraordinary ability to craft ideas. This book wouldn't have found its way to the store shelf without his efforts.

Bill Swallow provided the all-important feedback that kept this book on target. His insightful thinking paved the way for success.

Herb and Mona Bayles freely gave their time and attention to that always difficult task of editing.

Al Enamait contributed his brilliant insights into the business world.

Kevin Thomas provided so much of the foundation for this project to succeed.

And of course, Jennifer, who always demonstrated just how much good charisma can generate in the lives of others.

Contents

Creating the Charismatic Persona

1

THE CHARISMA FACTOR: THE POWER OF GRACEFUL INSPIRATION

Like the creative composer, some people are more gifted at living than others. They do have an effect on those around them, but the process stops there, because there is no way of describing in technical terms just what it is they do, most of which is out of awareness. Some time in the future, a long, long time from now when culture is more completely explored, there will be the equivalent of musical scores that can be learned, each for a different type of man or woman in different types of jobs and relationships, for time, space, work, and play. We see people who are successful and happy today, who have jobs which are rewarding and productive. What are the sets, isolates, and patterns that differentiate their lives from those of the less fortunate? We need to have a means for making life a little less haphazard and more enjoyable.

Edward T. Hall,
cultural anthropologist and intercultural communication
expert, in his book, *The Silent Language* (1959)

In each generation there are a few gifted individuals who capture the collective imagination. Because they inspire unswerving allegiance and devotion in so many, what they do seems almost to be magic. They have an extraordinary effect on others and the events of their time. What they create often takes on a life of its own, living on long after they are gone. These people possess what we have come to call charisma.

As Edward T. Hall noted, there has been no equivalent of "musical scores" we could follow, nothing from which we could learn what made these leaders different from others. Although we have appreciated and admired their song, we were unable to replicate its melody.

The vision which flowed through Hall's mind was, however, actually an accurate picture of a future not nearly as distant as he thought. Less than four decades later, we move closer to his dream. Even now, we can catch glimpses of the patterns marking certain people distinctive or exceptional.

The men and women profiled in this book led from their hearts. They had an amazing natural ability, an aptitude for the extraordinary. Their passion fueled achievements that changed lives. It also enabled them to bring others along on remarkable journeys.

Although many of them came to live in the high castles of popularity and power, their hearts always remained with those they led. They shared themselves out of an amazing generosity of spirit. All cared passionately for their vision. But they cared just as passionately for those involved in its realization.

Charismatic leaders illuminated much with their natural brilliance. Their leadership gave vision to those who would otherwise have remained blind. But we were so dazzled by *what* they did, we were unable to see *how* they did it. We can be thankful that science and research have finally caught up with the natural wonders by which these people lived and worked.

This book offers a view into the inner workings of the patterns comprising the phenomenon we call charisma. It is a blueprint for liberating yourself from the restrictions of procedures, regulations, and standard logic. It offers you an opportunity to become a natural leader. You can be a leader who creates exceptional results because you cause people to believe in their own promise.

This is the kind of leadership that allows you not only to move toward your own best possible future, but to draw others toward theirs. Once opened to the limitless realm of possibility and the infinite potential of human spirit, you can capture the hearts and minds of others.

The Charisma Factor creates the "musical score" for natural leadership. Follow it and the ability to lead and inspire the best in others can be yours. In today's increasingly complex and rapidly changing world, there is an outcry for effective leaders. Is there any reason you shouldn't be one of them?

DEFINING CHARISMA: PATTERNS OF GREATNESS

CHARISMA 1: A special quality of leadership that captures the popular imagination and inspires unswerving allegiance and devotion 2: a person who has some divinely inspired gift, grace, or talent 3: magnetic charm or appeal

The dictionary falls short in helping us understand charisma. Its words fail to capture the true essence of this leadership trait. Yes, charisma can ignite imagination and inspire devotion. But, it does far more than that. There are those who would agree it's a divine gift or magical property given to the few and the blessed. And there are still others who would tell you it's little more than sex appeal, which fascinates and beguiles. Its effects upon others indicated that charismatic leadership had to be more than charm and was certainly less than a divine gift visited upon the chosen. What then is it?

Originally, the word *charisma* was used in the religious sense. It described a speaking through one's soul, being set afire by the Holy Spirit. Then Max Weber, an early management theorist and a founder of modern sociology, borrowed the term to describe a type of leadership trait. It quickly moved into popular secular use.

Although we readily adopted the word, we remained uncertain about exactly *what* charisma was and *how* it worked. One thing was obvious: *People with charisma created a strong bond with those they lead.* Followers become impassioned in the causes of charismatic leaders. The followers have the desire to do the things these leaders want done.

> *Having charisma means you are able to touch the hearts and minds of those around you. You can move others into action.*

That one fact was the starting point. It took important breakthroughs in the understanding of neurological processing and the effects of language on human beings to lead us to an accurate definition of charisma. They led the way to a remarkable discovery: Charismatic leaders speak a sort of communicative code. Undeniably, *charisma is a form of communication.* Actually, it uses the one language capable of reaching every individual: the language of emotion.

Emotions drive human behavior. They overcome the many obstacles created by logical thought. *Those who can harness people's emotional energy consistently achieve outstanding results.* While others logically argue with the conscious mind, charismatic leaders are communicating with the soul. They stimulate in people the emotional drive, making others eager to do what needs to be done.

Charisma is actually a specialized set of communication techniques used by leaders to reach the hearts and minds of those who follow them. Because they manage emotions, charismatic leaders can bypass obstacles that hinder others. That is the real secret behind their phenomenal achievements. These communication techniques are not a rare gift but a natural part of being human. This means the seeds of charisma reside in all of us. They await only your cultivation.

THE CHARISMA FACTOR 7

CHARISMA: UNCOVERING THE MOST POWERFUL OF LEADERSHIP STRATEGIES

Successful leaders get all types of people with differing backgrounds, beliefs, and values to focus on a project in total synchrony. It's as though you're a symphony conductor with people as your instruments. Your vision is the symphony waiting to be brought to life. To do so requires you to draw precise human performance from others. It's your ability to inspire that will result in a virtuoso performance by each player.

Given the people and circumstances leaders sometimes face, this can seem impossible. Charismatic leaders not only do it, they make it look easy. You may have been told that in order to get things done you must convince, persuade, influence, negotiate, enjoin, or intimidate others. Yet these processes infrequently result in the outstanding results you seek. And when they do, they do so at the expense of good will.

On the other hand, people *want* to carry out the plans of the charismatic leader–often without being directly asked or assigned. Because charisma inspires loyalty and enthusiasm, everyone becomes allied in achievement. Using charismatic communication techniques, you no longer have to force or logically convince others to follow. They have a natural desire to do so. They naturally want the same things you do, *want* to do what you wish. You are able to infuse your vision into those around you. Your vision becomes the lightning rod for the limitless energy of human promise. It will soon sparkle and crackle with an electrical charge that brings it to life in the world.

Human beings haven't even begun to imagine all that is possible. Bound by conventional thought, most people never come close to fulfilling their highest potential. That means there are unused resources residing in everyone you lead. Think of what you could accomplish if you tapped into those resources. What if you could ignite and harness that potential, putting it to work? There is a key to people's talent.

Master the unique properties of charismatic communication and that key is in your hand.

It's important to realize that the Charisma Factor is a specific set of techniques being employed every day in all areas of life. This is not some alchemistic process used to transform people into automatons. It isn't found in dusty books hidden in dark corners of a secret library known only to the initiated. It's just that most people who use it do so naturally, out of their own conscious awareness. You may even use it yourself without knowing it.

Recognizing Charisma

Somewhere along the line we mislabeled charisma. We've been paying for that mistake with lost opportunities ever since. We generally have accepted that charisma is a gift bestowed only upon a special few. Since we believe chance or fate grants it to few individuals, we fail to nurture the seeds of charisma existing in all of us. Naturally charismatic leaders have long been showing us the way. Until now, however, no one has provided charisma's "musical score" for the rest of us to follow.

We have to begin thinking differently about charisma. It isn't something capriciously given or denied us. It isn't a nebulous concept or magic. It doesn't have to be rare. Charisma is a *way* of communicating, a process creating powerful reverberations in others. It's a skill you can develop and use.

What's taken us so long? If charismatic communication is a distinctive technology, why hasn't anyone identified it before? The problem begins with our failure to recognize or acknowledge certain things in our external world because of an internal bias we have. We thus create what is called a "perceptual barrier." When we say of someone, "He just doesn't get it," what we mean is, "He just doesn't see it." And he doesn't see it because some preconceived idea or belief blinds him to what is before his eyes. The belief says, "This thing does not exist." The eyes don't dispute the point.

For example, both formal and informal business learning has tended to teach the importance of looking at systems and theories when problems arise. The bias is toward things that can be broken down into numbers. Recently, more words are being spoken about considering people, but there remains far too little true understanding of the human factor in business.

During the 1970s into the early '80's MBO (Management by Objectives) became the rage for both the private and public sectors. It, like many of its predecessors, was hailed as *the* answer for achieving greater productivity. In fact, MBO was a logical and reasonable way to structure the resources of an organization. What it didn't take into account was the single most important element (the one so often missed by Western business): the individual worker.

It is a prerequisite for any leader to first define a direction and make sure his or her organization has the resources to accomplish it. There's where many stop, however. They believe that a well-written plan, a thoroughly laid-out course of action, ensures successful completion. After all, all people know what they are supposed to do. They've been told what to do and how to do it. So now they'll do it, right? Sometimes.

Here's where charismatic leaders step out in front of the pack. They don't just believe, wish, or hope others will pick up the ball and run with it. They *create* the enthusiasm, excitement, and motivation others need to jump into the game and begin playing their best. Many have been taught to correctly structure programs, policies, and game plans. A few have naturally known there were other steps to be taken. They went on to inspire others to their best efforts. They are the ones who achieved astonishing results.

It s surprising how much the behavior of people differs from theories about how they *should* act and react in the work place. No matter how wide the gap, too many managers continue to act as though it doesn't exist. Blinded to the reality of human nature, they regularly fall into the crevice of failed projects. Fished out and dusted off, they bone up on more theory before attempting another leap. Internally, their bias was set long ago. They fail to recognize the importance of human feeling to everything, including the bottom line they value so highly.

Yet, most often there are human factors behind all problems, including those of profitability. Let's suppose a small manufacturing company experiences a marked increase in product return and rapid escalation of sick days being used. The president responds with orders for tighter quality control measures, a time study, and an analysis of worker safety habits. He doesn't even think about the day two months ago when he pulled into the employee parking lot in a new luxury automobile. Neither does he recall this was just a week after the announcement of several layoffs due to the cancellation of a large contract.

Even if someone pointed this out, he still might not "get it." He'd wonder what his purchase could possibly have to do with employee productivity. The last thing he would consider taking into account in analyzing the problem is basic human nature. Besides, he'd say, the car had been ordered months before, and he had several sound business reasons for buying it.

So we stumble along, occasionally tripping over things we refuse to see because our internal beliefs say they don't exist. It's no wonder we haven't recognized the charismatic communication occurring right before our eyes. Our limited conscious awareness of the all-important human feelings has blurred our vision and understanding. Then, to make things worse, we've been saddled with cultural training that in effect creates a blind spot. The real wonder is that we ever get anywhere at all.

WHY YOU WILL KNOW WHAT OTHERS DON'T

How we act and react depends not so much on *what occurs around us* as on *how we perceive it*. We are constantly assaulted by a glut of information on what we are seeing, hearing, smelling, feeling, or touching. The problem is our conscious mind has limited processing ability. It can take in only a small amount of all the available sensory information.

There's only one thing our conscious mind can do about this. It must *select* what it will grasp and process. The first and most important criterion it uses in this selection process is *what the mind considers important at that moment*. This means we pay no conscious attention to things having no apparent significance to our current experience.

For example, as you read the previous sentence you were not consciously aware of the feeling in your right big toe, the sound of your breathing, or the objects within the limits of your peripheral vision. But as you just read those words, your mind may have momentarily shifted focus to each of those elements. If it didn't then, it has now.

This is important information. Because our mind *must* select what it will mentally seize and process, *humans have only a limited grasp of their total experience*. Most of what goes on around us occurs out of our conscious realization. When we communicate with others, they can consciously focus on only a small portion of what we say. So they screen out components considered unimportant to them. This means the message *we* want or need to deliver may be effectively distorted. To make matters worse, listeners then associate and interpret the part of the message they did receive in ways we never even considered.

We've all led meetings, given speeches, or had conferences where what people left with was something distinctly different from what we intended to deliver. On the personal front, we've all had an important talk with a spouse or friend in which what we said and what they heard were two completely different things. What seemed apparent and simple to us became complicated and incomprehensible in the mind of our partner.

This problem is not particular to a certain sex, profession, or social class. It is simply part of being human. When we process something we have seen or heard, our mind calls up memories that *in its judgment* are similar in nature and meaning. These internal representations are filters through which we sift current experience. Each person's memories are as unique as that person's fingerprints. So everyone's filters are different from everyone else's. No two people will interpret the same experience in exactly the same way.

Have you ever heard (or been one half of) a couple relating an incident that sounded as if they were talking about two different events? They may even argue heatedly over what actually did or did not occur. It's obvious they have completely different memories of the same incident. And each is dead certain his or her version is "true," what "really" happened.

> *Much of what occurs around us happens out of our awareness, yet continues to have a substantial impact on us.*

What we are convinced "really" happened is actually the "reality" we created by individually selecting what we would consciously see, hear, and feel. "Reality" is a distilled product, the end result of our conscious mind's filtering process. We thus create our own personal model of the world, our own version of reality.

The process we use to create our understanding of an experience is like composing a photograph through the lens of a camera. Our mind can place some things in and others out of focus. It can zoom in on one item and effectively exclude everything else. Or the lens can be pulled back to view a larger part of the surroundings. The resulting picture represents a certain view of a time and place. It is a memory, something far different from the actual total occurrence.

Reading the Fine Print of Human Behavior

Our culture has played an important role in keeping the meaning of charisma a secret. It teaches us to direct our limited focus toward certain things and to overlook others. We analyze the words of charismatic leaders and attempt to make judgments about things like their "presence," "eye contact," or "leadership quality."

Charismatic communication has remained a mystery because it deals with such subtle realms of human interaction. They are ones to which we are perceptually blinded. Our beliefs say, "These things don't exist." Our cultural training (especially in the business world) has instructed us to focus on policies, procedures, and techniques—the "real" stuff. We don't have a lot of time for people and concepts. If we consider them at all, it is in a broad, sweeping manner.

On the other hand, we are taught to dissect the technical in minute detail. After all, these things have been defined as "tangible." Meanwhile, we overlook the human subtleties, which are just as real. They are like delicately spun webs whose intricate beauty is passed daily by hundreds of people walking along a well-worn path. Because most people choose not to see this marvel of nature does not mean it doesn't exist.

Our culture places an incredibly high reliance on the spoken word. It's real. To Westerners it is thought to be the primary form of human interaction and communication. The fact that we now know words comprise only a small fraction of human communication hasn't changed this belief.

Other cultures place less emphasis on the spoken word. They wisely combine the use of words with other elements of the human communicative process. As you will discover in the following chapters, those with charisma use words in ways that distract the attention of the conscious mind. This frees them to communicate extraverbally with the unconscious minds of listeners. This is charismatic communication.

We are also trained to create an almost immediate impression about people. To do so, we must view human behavior in large chunks. We watch for and judge such things as the firmness of a handshake, the amount of eye contact, and the depth of a voice. This makes it difficult, if not impossible, to understand why certain people have such a striking effect on others. It's like trying to put together a jigsaw puzzle blindfolded. You might get lucky and actually do it, but it's going to be difficult.

We know that human beings are complex creatures. This doesn't stop us from making permanent judgments about them based on trivial information. Interestingly, we spend far more time and effort reviewing a contract word for word than reading the fine print of human behavior. But it's this human fine print that makes far more difference in the day-to-day successes and failures of our lives. Charismatic communication is part of the fine print of human behavior. It's not that it is a nebulous concept. It's just that we have been blinded to it.

The simple reason charisma has been such a difficult concept to replicate is that its foundation lies outside culturally created boundaries. Its components are not part of the information we have been taught to be consciously aware of. The cultural boundaries of our experience direct our focus away from the factors of charismatic communication. It's much like a telescope at a scenic viewpoint that has been set to direct onlookers' perspectives onto a specific view and is incapable of being turned to another direction. In this way, culture guides what we consciously see on our walk through life.

You are being asked to adjust the lens of your focus. As you read this book, search and explore your memories at new levels. Recall the times you were exposed to a charismatic leader. As we break down and discuss the individual elements of charismatic communication, break down and review the memories of what you saw and heard. You will begin to see how those subtle but powerful techniques affected you.

This is not the way most of us are accustomed to remembering. For example, if you were to recall something like a summer vacation, you would usually think in large pieces. You'd run the whole trip through your mind, often stopping at certain places or days that were especially memorable. You'd completely overlook the thousands of minute experiences cumulatively creating these memories. There were things like the feel of a child's hand grasping yours in fearful wonder as a deer nibbled corn from her other hand. Or the pulsating rhythm of waves slapping and rocking your boat while the warm sun soaked into your weary body. There are cultures where thinking in such fashion is common. Our Western teaching avoids such precise processing, believing it inefficient at best and maddening at worst.

Total span
of human
communication

Realm of charismatic communication

Culturally restricted perceptions

INSPIRING GREATNESS: THE KEY TO CHARISMA

The secret at the heart of charismatic communication is simple: *Human beings are emotionally driven creatures*. Human behavior and levels of performance are based more on how we *feel* than on the rational or logical consequences of what we do.

We all understand how sometimes we are "in the mood" to do something and other times we are not. We also know how *the mood we are in greatly affects the efficiency and quality of our work*. Think about times you were really "cooking." The report you wrote, the presentation you gave, the meeting you led just flowed effortlessly. It probably remains one of the best you've ever done. We all have days where we *feel* as though we are unstoppable. The funny thing about it is, when we *feel* unstoppable, we usually are.

So what happens when we *feel* inspired? Usually, we naturally do outstanding work, because we are in the appropriate *emotional* state of mind for it. We have a strong natural desire to get the job done. On the other hand, we've all had to write a report, give a presentation, or lead a meeting when we didn't feel much like doing it. We were feeling things such as fatigue, depression, discouragement, or boredom. What happened then? Chances are we not only had a more difficult time performing, but the results were less than our best.

We can see how emotions drive human behavior, performance, and excellence. They create energy and action. If emotionally we are feeling something other than the states needed to effectively and efficiently perform the job, emotions become barriers to high-level performance. All too often what is inhibiting our performance isn't lack of talent or ability. It's simply not being in the necessary emotional state to do our best.

For us to be at our best in any endeavor we must be in the corresponding and appropriate emotional state of mind. Too many people think of emotions in terms of intense levels or extremes such as overwhelming sorrow, joy, or gripping fear. Most often discrete and subtle emotional states *are what govern high performance*. When we talk about emotions in this book we most often mean what many would refer to as "moods."

"I'm in a great mood!"

"I'm really in the mood to work."

"I'm just not in the mood to do anything today."

These are all things we've heard and said. It's these more subtle emotional states that direct performance and actions.

Charismatic leaders are aware of and use emotional states. In fact, the ability to reach people at the emotional level is at the core of charismatic communication. Some special leaders have always *intuitively* known what science has now come to know. *People must be naturally stimulated emotionally if they are to be led into action.*

These leaders didn't try to convince others of their cause. Rather, they *inspired the emotions* that would naturally lead others to share their goals. Charismatic leaders incite the best in people, making others want to follow rather than needing to coax or threaten others. This is important. Should people *feel* dedicated they will stay the course. Should they *feel* excited about a goal they will happily devote their best efforts to securing it. Should they *feel* confident they will risk their best.

If you have ever tried to convince a smoker or drinker to stop, you know that every logical argument about health, family, profession, or anything else does no good. Surprisingly, a number of the same people upon whom begging, bribing, threatening, or cajoling have no effect will sometime later make a decision to stop. And they do, no matter what effort it takes. Although each will give a different reason for finally quitting, these decisions will have one thing in common. Each decision is based upon a motivation that is emotionally compelling to them.

That's why charismatic leaders use communicative techniques that focus on the emotional state of others rather than depending upon the success of logical argument. They use the emotional states of others as the fuel of human excellence. These leaders don't just tell people what they want done. They ignite others' deepest capabilities, enabling them to perform with excellence and dedication.

This is not to say that they manipulate others. The communication skills outlined in this book do create acceptance as a leader. They will not, however, turn you into a sort of Svengali able to con others into doing all sorts of things they don't want to do. To use charismatic communication in leadership you must be proficient in all the techniques in this book. These techniques include a strong ethical component, built-in safeguards. Those attempting to circumvent or screen out the ethical considerations will find themselves with an incomplete package. They may be successful at simulating charismatic leadership for awhile. But, it's like covering something dirty with a coat of white paint. It doesn't take long for the grime to bleed through or the clean veneer to crack, exposing the soiled surface beneath. Ethical leadership and charismatic communication go hand and hand. To separate one from the other ensures ultimate failure. Combining the two enables you to do more for yourself and others than you ever dreamed possible.

THE SECRET THAT CREATES ACTION

Human beings want certain feelings more than they want anything else. Think about it. Do you really want a new car or a bigger home? Or do you want the feelings you think come with driving a new car, living in a big house? Is it one million dollar bills you want to win in the lottery? Or is it the lure of freedom or security money can give that keeps you buying those tickets? Taking it a step further: It may not even be freedom or security you want but the feelings you think they will give you.

Feelings are powerful. They quickly create or change attitudes and beliefs. They often have a lasting effect on what happens between people. *Charismatic leaders are those who induce specific feelings and emotions in people by the way they speak, move, and act.* Ronald Reagan and John F. Kennedy had a way of making people *feel* as though everything was under control and the government was in the hands of strong leadership. It didn't matter what their speeches contained in the way of substance. They communicated with their listeners through how they made others *feel*.

> *Charismatic leaders provide the commodity of feelings and emotions to their audiences. When you give people the feelings they strive for, you are fulfilling their deepest desires.*

If behavior is based on emotional state, what creates emotions? "Internal focus" is recognized as one of the dominant factors controlling human emotions. Internal focus is what people are thinking at a given time: their thoughts.

Stanford University studies have shown that thinking about an experience activates the nervous system the same way the actual experience does. This means *the emotional state of human beings shifts in response to what they focus upon.* When we think about positive experiences we move toward resourceful and positive emotional states. The reverse is also true. Dwelling upon negative experiences generates nonproductive emotions as long as our focus remains there.

Think about a time you had an unpleasant experience at the office. Let's say an important client or your boss lashed out at you for something out of your control or not your responsibility. What happened as you drove home? Did you replay the scene over and over in your head, hearing his voice almost like a needle stuck on a record? What happened to your state? If you couldn't "let go" of the incident and continued to replay it, did you have a pleasant evening? Were you an enjoyable companion? Probably not.

As you continued to focus on the event, you probably became even more upset. Of course, the reverse would be true. If you had focused upon a positive or happy experience, your state would have become more resourceful. As you replayed that positive scene, you would have continued to feel better.

> *Everyone's behavior is very much directed by his or her emotional state of mind. Charismatic communicators direct the emotional state of their audience, thus communicating more effectively and guiding others into action.*

On a visit to a retirement home, we struck up a conversation with an elderly resident. Asked how she was feeling, she responded in a low and shaky voice. Her eyes remained focused on the floor as she recounted her ailments and pains. A few minutes later, we noticed numerous pictures of her grandchildren carefully arranged on her bureau. We changed the conversation by asking, "So tell us, which one of your grandchildren makes you laugh the most?" As she sorted through her fondest memories, her eyes began to sparkle. Her face lost its grimace and a smile grew. She sat up straight. The remainder of our conversation was lively and upbeat.

When asked questions that directed her thoughts, the woman changed her emotional state of mind in a matter of seconds. The simple asking of two questions steered her thoughts toward memories that were charged with emotions. The first reminded her of her many discomforts. The second recalled happy and enjoyable memories of her grandchildren.

> *If you can aim the thoughts of others, you can direct their emotional state. Guide their emotions and you guide their actions.*

EMOTIONAL ENERGY:
WHEN LOGIC ISN'T ENOUGH

There are medical patients who suffer from one of many severe neurological disorders that destroy substantial brain function. They will often sit motionless for hours. Seemingly catatonic, these individuals apparently don't experience any impulse to move, to take even the smallest action. This condition is called *aboulia*.

From a neurological perspective, aboulia is characterized by a lack of will or, more precisely, a paralysis of the will. Yet many of these patients who could remain completely statuelike or flaccid for long periods would eat, walk, or communicate with just a little assistance.

In some cases, if someone just slipped an arm as a guide through theirs, they would stand and walk anywhere with the other person. But if this light connection was broken, they would fall limply to the floor where they stayed indefinitely. Others would stare blankly at a meal, making no movement on their own. However, it sometimes required only a slight nudge on their fork to cause them to begin eating (Sacks, 1990). In recent experiments, teenagers afflicted with severe autism were able to communicate coherently by typing on a computer *as long as someone lifted their arms and placed them over the keyboard*.

In each case, individuals with aboulia were able to perform tasks *as long as they could borrow the will of someone else*. For whatever reason, they lacked the will, the initiative, to begin the task themselves. We all suffer from aboulia of sorts. At one time or another, everyone lacks the enthusiasm, excitement, or discipline to see a job through. Other times, feelings like fear, anger, or apathy keep us from advancing, or even just taking that next step in life.

Whatever the reason, there are times we, as well as those we lead, lack the basic *emotional will* to do a good job. Corporate America loses billions each year because people simply lack the will to follow through, the will to keep going. What does this have to do with charismatic leadership?

In its simplest sense, leaders set forth a goal, the direction of an organization. They define the basic steps for everyone to take and say, "Go to it." Charismatic leaders set forth a goal, the direction of an organization. They also define the basic steps for everyone to take, but then they do something different. They *then infuse within everyone the emotional will, the emotional energy to excitedly and enthusiastically follow through with the goal.* Charismatic leaders spark in people the drive that ensures their best efforts.

Charismatic leaders actually coordinate the performance of others by employing the tools of *emotional management.* The problem for most people is that in school they learned to systematically analyze the world around them in a reasoning fashion. They learned to use linear logic. This is an important form of logic, necessary and useful. Managers, whose performance is usually based upon a quantitative measure such as "the bottom line" need linear-oriented logic as a basis for making decisions in a standardized fashion.

In this way logic serves managers well. It does little or nothing, however, toward developing and directing high levels of performance in those they lead. Humans *are emotionally* driven. To get the best out of people, to bring them to action, we must communicate in that realm. The effective leader must strategically communicate a vision and assist others in changing their behavior to achieve that vision. Logic is no help here.

Why logic doesn't work well in getting others to take action is that *logic isn't universal.* Each of us has his or her own personal "system" of logic. Of course, there is a good deal of overlap from person to person. But the parts most important to motivating people into action are usually unique. We each have internal criteria for knowing what is good and what is bad, when we should work hard and when it's okay to slack off, when to move ahead with a plan and when to hold off, when to buy and when not to, and so on. Each day we make hundreds of decisions. *We literally have thousands of unique criteria embedded into our neurology that tell us when to and when not to do, say, or believe something.*

For example, success is really nothing more than a *feeling*. There are times in our lives when we *feel* successful about certain endeavors and other times when we don't. The difference is that our personal criteria for success is being met at certain times, so we *feel* successful at only those times.

For example, let's pretend that to *feel* successful in life John's personal criteria say he must (1) hold a prominent position overseeing at least 100 people, (2) own a certain style house in a particular neighborhood, (3) have the means to send his children to an Ivy League university, and (4) hold season tickets for the local professional football team and the opera.

This doesn't mean John is consciously aware of his criteria or ever articulates them. These things are established somewhat haphazardly over time and often remain unknown at the conscious level. Still, John will only *feel* totally successful as long as all four of these criteria are met. Should he meet only three, he would *feel* marginally successful. Should he meet only one or two, he probably won't *feel* very good about his success in life, no matter what else he had or achieved.

Criteria are important to human functioning. Criteria allow us to shift through all the information racing into our brains at any time and greatly assist us in decision making. We may have anywhere from one to eight criteria governing a given area of life. When our criteria are met, the brain fires off the emotional response necessary for us to take action. Should our perceptions tell us our criteria have not been sufficiently met, we will not be compelled to act accordingly.

For example, let's suppose you want to hire away the ace marketing director from your main competitor. You invite her to lunch and lay out what your company has to offer her. You proudly tell her about the outstanding benefits package you offer, the large salary increase, the increased staff she will have working for her, and the long-term growth potential of your company. You are very excited about these things, because they are what is important to you. They meet your criteria for an irresistible job offer. Yet, despite what you consider a very impressive offer, you note only mild interest on her part. You wonder why she is not jumping at such an opportunity. Later, she rejects your offer. What went wrong?

Probably you met only a few of *her* personal criteria for moving to a new job.

Your Enticements

1. Company Benefits
2. Salary
3. Large Staff
4. Growth of Company

Her Criteria

1. Good Benefits
2. Personal Growth
3. Aggressive Marketing Posture
4. Creative Freedom

As you can see, only one of her criteria for moving into a new position was met in your presentation. Therefore, she had little interest in the position. Perhaps your company also offers the other three, but because they are not important to you, you didn't mention them. Had you been fortunate enough to say the right things, you would have met her criteria. The offer would automatically have reached the appropriate neurological networks in her brain, activating the *feeling* in her that making the move was the right thing to do. Once she had the "right feeling," she would probably have accepted your offer.

When you want someone to take a certain action and you don't know his or her personal criteria, your job is that much more difficult. When you need to do this, not with one but with large numbers of people, the task can become monumental. What makes the job even more difficult is that each of our thousands of criteria have been embedded in haphazard fashion. For most of us there is little rhyme or reason to them.

What was designed to assist us in decision making may actually hinder a productive decision-making process. Unknown to us, these sets of criteria keep us from functioning at our highest levels. Do you wonder what your specific criteria are for a given area of life? The process to figure it out is quite simple. It doesn't matter if the personal criteria you want to determine are for being successful, purchasing a product, falling in love, or knowing when an employee is doing a good job. The question you ask is still the same. "What has to happen for me to . . .?" Complete it with "Be successful," "Make a purchase," "Be in love," "Feel satisfied with an employee's performance," or whatever. Now, write down all the criteria that come to mind. This is even simpler if you recall a similar event in your past as you answer the question.

So, what about charismatic communicators? Don't they have to deal with individual sets of criteria too? How do they get people to accept their ideas with enthusiasm, buy their merchandise, or comfortably follow them through stringent difficulties? Aren't they governed and limited by the same constraints as the rest of us are? NO!

Charismatic communicators bypass the criteria stage of information processing. They deal directly with the emotional impulses driving behavior. They know how to move past the "logical" constraints of the conscious mind and give people the strong desire to take action. They deal directly with emotions, the fuel of human performance and excellence.

For example, during a presentation to raise money for a nonprofit organization, a fund raiser will make suggestions encouraging a donation. To be successful, the presentation must meet the criteria that will motivate that individual to donate. Once the criteria are met, the person's mind automatically ignites the specific feelings that make him or her naturally take action and donate. The process would look like this:

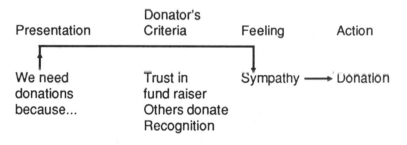

	Donator's		
Presentation	Criteria	Feeling	Action
We need donations because...	→ Trust in fund raiser Others donate Recognition	→ Sympathy	→ Donation

Charismatic communicators soliciting donations would use a different set of techniques, completely bypassing the criteria stage. These people would focus on eliciting the emotion of sympathy rather than on attempting to go through the maze of criteria. In this way those being asked to donate will naturally want to donate and may even be compelled to do so. The process would look like this:

	Donator's		
Presentation	Criteria	Feeling	Action
We need donations because...	Trust in fund raiser Others donate Recognition	Sympathy → Donation	

Charismatic communication is a distinct process with its own rules and its own logical progression. Leaders using charismatic communication follow three steps in specific order. Charismatic impact is created in others when each step is firmly established before the leader moves to the next.

In this book, you will learn to move through these steps in sequence. As you master them, you will begin to powerfully and subtly draw people toward you. You will ignite their desire to do exactly what you want them to—without even asking. The process we call the Charisma Factor has been developed from some of history's greatest charismatic leaders. It is the "musical score" of their greatness, one you can learn and then play to create the symphony of your greatest successes.

Step 1

The specific persona, almost an aura, around those special leaders possessing charisma is part of a specific communication process. They communicate with others with their whole being rather than just with words. A powerful presence is created when the entire spectrum of the human communication band is used. By using a few simple techniques that you will learn, these leaders create a communicative impact many times more powerful than that of anyone around them. This is the foundation of charismatic communication. It must be in place and maintained at all times for you to have a charismatic impact.

Step 2

Before even attempting leadership, people with charisma draw others in. They create a link that engenders a desire to follow their leadership. What they do is develop an actual neurological connection. It is this connection that creates strong feelings of affinity and trust. You may have seen these skills in action. They result in what has been referred to as the "likability factor." This occurs when people accept, like, and respect you for who you are. Once you learn how to form this link, people will naturally view you as a leader they want to follow.

Step 3

The hallmark of charismatic leaders is their ability to inspire and manage virtually any emotion in those around them. When filled with their best feelings, people naturally want to take action. They willingly follow established leadership in any ethical direction. The tools of emotional management can be applied in any situation or interaction, from enhancing personal relationships to increasing sales. They focus not so much on the logical flow of points or ideas but on the flow of emotions within others. Emotional management is the final step in moving others to action.

In Short

1. **Charisma isn't so much a gift as it is a specific form of communication. It is the language of emotion.**
2. **Charisma is the ability to spark emotion in others. In fact, charisma could be considered the ability to inspire others to action. This is important because human beings are emotionally driven creatures. If you want to create drive, motivation, and enthusiasm in others you must touch them emotionally, not logically.**
3. **Charismatic communication is the three-step process that the great charismatic leaders have all used to harness the best from their employees, clients, and supporters.**
4. **Charismatic leadership is highly learnable because it is a process rather than a function of personality.**

2

THE CHARISMATIC PERSONA

We watch and listen to charismatic leaders, admiring their boldness, moved by their power. There's something in their magnetic presence. It seems to melt potential opposition like the first snowflakes of winter dissolving on earth still warm from autumn's sun. Even more important, under these leaders' guidance people feel their own power and potential stir and come to life.

Charismatic leaders seem always in command of their environment. Yet others do not feel intimidated or fearful of them. Rather, followers feel welcomed. They comfortably move into the warmth of the charismatic leader's circle. Followers feel in partnership with the leader. Because everyone knows they are an essential part of the group, they are passionately committed. Anything becomes possible.

In this section we explore just how the charismatic persona unleashes greatness. We also reveal how you can achieve the same level of influence as some of the greatest leaders. In this chapter we begin with a look at the common traits of charismatic leaders and tell you how you can pre-program yourself for success.

It's easy to see *what* charismatic leaders do. The effect they have on others and the successes of their lives are apparent. What isn't so easy to understand is *how* they do it. We can see the result, but the process has remained cloaked in mystery and myth. In fact, until recently we weren't sure there was a step-by-step procedure to be identified and taught to others. Charisma was or it wasn't. People had it or they didn't. Or, so we thought.

Part of the mystery has been that a close look at charismatic leaders reveals first their differences. What they achieve, where and when they live and work, their politics, ethnicity, values, who follows them, and why they are beloved all are distinct. But if charisma is something definable and teachable then, despite the apparent differences, all these leaders had to share something. They did.

Charismatic leaders use charisma differently. But, they all share several common traits that are the framing for their successes. Because we focus on the deeds and personal differences of these leaders, the traits remain invisible. It's not unlike admiring the distinctiveness of a house. We never see the framing holding it up. Yet, without framing, even the most beautiful house collapses into a heap of random building materials.

If you want to develop a charismatic persona, you must commit yourself to its construction. This book is your blueprint. But only you can provide the framework upon which to build. Without this framework of traits, the techniques taught in this book will remain merely useful materials piled on a construction site.

TAKING THE HIGH GROUND

Charismatic leaders share a strikingly similar outlook on life and leadership. For them,, both are wonderful and positive challenges. In fact, leadership is a natural part of their lives. And life itself is an adventure that excites and inspires.

You don't find charismatic leaders entrenched behind barricades. They never allow problems to hold them down or count them out. These leaders are active, continuously moving forward. Their movements are never random. Because their movements are directed and precise, they often lead to startling successes. Charismatic leaders do more than see the glass as half full. They eagerly plan the filling of it to overflowing. In other words, *charismatic leaders are optimists*.

If you want charisma, sharing this positive perspective is essential. *To be a charismatic leader, you must be the kind of person who never gives up.* You too must constantly search for new ways to reach goals. This attitude is never more important than when problems rear up. It doesn't matter if it is the first or the fiftieth sign of trouble. As a leader, your first job is to keep yourself and everyone around you moving toward the goal.

There's nothing inspirational in halting everyone's momentum so they can stand and stare at the obstacles. Ever hear a story about a great leader who shrugged his or her shoulders and said, "Oh well, at least we tried," before leading his or her followers into full retreat? Of course not. This is not what legends are made of.

To have a magnetic leadership presence you must first maintain an optimistic view of yourself, your leadership, and your goal. In truth, an optimistic thinking style is the glue holding together the entire technology of the Charisma Factor. At its core, much of charisma has to do with making people feel good, empowering them to do their best. And people doing their best is what leads to high levels of achievement.

We are only in the beginning stages of fully understanding the powerful effects mental attitude has on us. We do know that people like optimists and enjoy being around them. In contrast, we generally avoid pessimists whenever we can. And small wonder, when most often we actually feel ourselves sink lower in the depressing and smothering presence of the gloomy thinker.

Do not confuse optimism with denying reality. True optimists see the world as it is. It's just that they know there are always options to get what they want—*if* they want it badly enough. Optimists know new routes can always be found, no matter how bleak the current situation. Because optimists *believe* they can make things better, they *can* make things better.

The most valuable characteristic of optimism is how powerfully it impacts the behavior of others. When we have taken the high ground, especially during difficult times, it has a transforming power. The positive energy we create is like a magnetic field. It pulls everyone together and toward us—even (or especially) those most uncertain and fearful.

Results from in-depth studies on how pessimistic and optimistic thinking influence people and their lives have rendered some striking results. In one investigation, it was found that the more optimistic the presidential candidate, the more apt he was to win the election. *In a review of the last ten presidential campaigns, it was found that the more optimistic candidate won in nine out of the ten races.* (Seligman, 1990)

Additionally, the more optimistic the candidate was in comparison to his opponent, the greater the margin he won by. In the one race where the optimistic candidate didn't win, he had been adversely affected early on by circumstances outside his control. Seligman's calculations indicated the candidate would probably have won if he'd had three more days to campaign.[1]

Campaign speeches reviewed for what had been identified as optimistic and pessimistic linguistic statements found that

---

[1] In 1966 Hubert Humphrey's race against Richard Nixon was adversely affected by riots outside the Democratic convention in Chicago. American viewers watched on national television as police beat demonstrators. Humphrey's popularity plummeted. Still, despite being fifteen points behind in the polls, Humphrey aggressively led his campaign on a rally. The effort carried him within 1 percent of the popular vote on election day.

... the more pessimistic candidate should engender less hope in the voters. The permanent and pervasive statements that pessimists make about bad events signal hopelessness. The more the candidate ruminates, the more this hopelessness is conveyed. If voters want a president who makes them believe he will solve the country's problems, they will choose the optimist.

This doesn't mean optimistic leaders ignore or deny problems. That would be neglecting one of the most important functions of leadership. Make no mistake about it: Optimistic leaders do address difficulties and problems. It is the way they talk about trouble that makes all the difference.

Optimistic leaders never discuss difficulties in permanent terms but always in finite terms. "Sure problems exist," admit optimistic leaders. "But they will not exist for long on *my* watch," they conclude. Once such leaders define a problem, they quickly move on to their plans for dealing with it.

In 1981 President Ronald Reagan faced the worst economic crisis of his tenure. In his address to the nation on the state of the economy, he immediately acknowledged the problem at hand. He then defined it in finite terms and began talking about the solution.

Good Evening.

I'm speaking to you tonight to give you a report on the state of our nation's economy. I regret to say that we're in the worst economic mess since the Great Depression.

A few days ago I was presented with a report I'd asked for, a comprehensive audit, if you will, of our economic condition. You won't like it. I didn't like it. But we have to face the truth and then go to work to turn things around. And make no mistake about it, we can turn them around. (Reagan, 1989)

Reagan's speech began the largest peacetime economic expansion in our nation's history.

Optimism and pessimism aren't difficult to understand. They are simply ways of thinking. We learn to think one way or the other. This means, of course, we can unlearn ways of thinking that don't serve us well. In truth, pessimistic thinking does nothing for any of us—and no one less so than a leader.

Pessimistic leaders spend much of their time focusing on existing problems or those they fear will arise. As with all human beings, *what they think about affects their attitudes.* There is a hammer of impending or possible problems constantly pounding in their brains. It drowns out the quiet voice within calmly offering options to any situation.

Pessimism is a caustic thought process. It can render us helpless by eating away at confidence and hope. Worse, it prevents us from assessing and choosing among the many tools and talents available to us. Pessimistic leaders' message and leadership style become as restricted and negative as their thoughts. Worst of all, they impregnate their followers with the demon twins of fear and despair.

In contrast, optimistic leaders are on a never-ending search for new and better ways to get things done. They know that once unleashed, the human spirit is capable of extraordinary achievement. Because they trust in their will to prevail, optimistic leaders don't sit down to mourn the difficulty of a situation. They just keep searching for ways to get beyond it. Faith in their eventual success makes them willing to tackle problems head-on. In fact, they relish the challenge. Their style of thinking keeps them, their followers, and their organizations moving forward with positive momentum.

Remember, optimistic leaders

- always phrase things in terms of what can be done or will be done.

- immediately address all problems and define them in finite terms.

- always provide a clear-cut course of action.

PASSION: IGNITING THE FLAME
OF YOUR SOUL

Another personal trait of charismatic leaders is passion for what they do. Passion moves and inspires, motivating others with its energy. With their directed passion, charismatic leaders are able to convince one, ten, or thousands to believe that anything is possible.

Anyone wanting to inspire others must have passion, because if you do not burn with energy, dedication, and love for what you do, how can you kindle a fire in others? Abraham Lincoln, John F. Kennedy, Dr. Martin Luther King, Jr., and Susan B. Anthony were all passionate leaders. Their styles differed markedly, yet within all of them welled a passion that poured out with every word from their mouth.

We have all suffered through listening to would-be leaders who had no zeal. Despite what might have been a polished style and delivery, something was missing. Perhaps we couldn't even say what it was. Maybe it was the tone of voice, the expression on their face, or the look in their eyes. Whatever it may have been—something communicated their lack of enthusiasm.

However it's communicated, an absence of passion will prevent you from moving people into action. If you have little emotion for a subject don't try to inspire passion in your audience. You will fail every time. *Passion is the catalyst for generating interest or enthusiasm.* Without it, the charismatic leader is merely a speaker, not unlike hundreds of others who toss words like darts, hoping one will hit the bull's eye of the listeners' enthusiasm.

Passion is precious because the day-to-day lives of most people lack it. Too many people walk around with a quiet hunger they may not even recognize. Because their own lives contain little, if any, emotional stimulation, people flock to action movies and follow flamboyant murder trials with gusto. They are drawn to the scenes of disasters where they gape at death and destruction hoping to stir the embers within them. What they are seeking is intensity of feeling.

Although they miss it, people fail to develop passion in their lives, because they are afraid. They worry about out-of-control passion consuming them. It can. Unbridled passion, like uncontrolled fire, can lead to chaos and destruction. But directed passion fuels with its flames the forge upon which dreams can be shaped.

As a leader, you want followers with passion. It continues to tip the scales in your favor, because people with passion continue pursuing the dream when others give up. Their deep love and dedication creates in them an unlimited drive. It provides unstoppable energy that hurtles them past any barrier. It keeps them up late at night and gets them out of bed early.

Lee Iacocca has passion. It was a major factor in his ability to shape Chrysler workers into a team capable of transforming a listless corporate giant into a vibrant, thriving company. His undaunted energy for a dream enabled him to lead vast numbers toward one goal. Each person at Chrysler was an individual shaped and colored by his or her own life. Each remained an individual but became united in the artistically designed mosaic of Iacocca's dream: a new Chrysler Corporation.

EXERCISE

Think of three things you are passionately committed to. How can you get that same level of commitment in other areas of your life?

When something is obviously important to someone, we naturally want to know more about it. That's why if you speak with true passion, others listen. They can't help it. They wonder if they're missing out on something crucial to their lives. Is there something vital in this for them? Passion in someone else leads others to consider their own stance. When someone facing execution says, "Give me liberty or give me death," others have to rethink their level of commitment to a cause.

If you have or develop passion, you can combine it with the technology taught in this book to make your leadership, presentations, work, and life more effective than you've ever dreamed. People will gather around you. They will listen and draw closer. Allow your passion to spill over into others' lives and they will see you as a bright burning flame. They will then naturally gather close to you, like someone seeking to warm cold hands at a fire.

THE EXTRAVERBAL LANGUAGE OF CHARISMA

Charismatic leaders are distinguished from most other leaders by how they communicate with others. More than vocalizing a message, these leaders embody it. They allow their presence to enthusiastically "speak" for them.

Do not confuse this with the trite "body language" of pop psychology fame. We aren't talking about leaders folding their arms a certain way or how and when they cross their legs. Do all charismatic leaders sit in the same positions and make the same movements? Obviously, they don't. In fact, charismatic leaders are all unique individuals. They copy or mimic no one.

Body language is comprised of those movements or gestures over which we have a certain level of conscious control. This includes things like the firmness of your handshake, the erectness of your posture, or the amount of eye contact. These behaviors do have an effect. But it's insignificant when compared to Charismatic Communication, a dynamic communication process using the entire physiology and neurology of the human body.

When we use Charismatic Communication, we speak with our whole being, not just with our mouth. And our message impacts the whole being of others, not just the language centers of the brain. Yet, for all we hear about body language, most people remain completely unaware of the far more complex and powerful Charismatic Communication. We don't have to be aware of it for our entire bodies to communicate messages from us to others. Only those who consciously use Charismatic Communication, however, ensure the messages received by others are those they want sent.

Charismatic Communication is so powerful because our person tells people far more than our words ever can. As extensive research has shown that only 7 percent of the message we receive comes through the words spoken. Thirty-eight percent is derived from vocal quality or *how* the words are being said. This includes the volume, tone, and tempo of the voice. The remaining 55 percent of the message comes through physiology (Mehrabian & Ferris, 1967). This means *things like posture, breathing rate, gestures, and eye movements communicate most of our message at the unconscious level.*

Unfortunately, most people remain focused almost completely on the words they are using when attempting to influence others. If you use this conventional method of communication, *you cut your ability to succeed by 93 percent.* On the other hand, using Charismatic Communication enables you to take advantage of the total communicative interaction between people.

Dr. Oliver Sacks, renowned clinical neurologist and author of the book *Awakenings,* is one of the country's most lucid writers on neurological disorders and their consequences. In a section of his book *The Man Who Mistook His Wife for a Hat,* Dr. Sacks profiles people afflicted with sensory aphasia. These individuals no longer understood the meaning of words due to lesions on the left hemisphere of their brains.

While they could clearly *hear* words being spoken, the words possessed no any meaning. Words became merely sounds. Imagine turning your television to a broadcast from a foreign country. If the program was in a language you neither spoke nor understood, the words would be sounds giving you no clue as to their meaning.

Despite their devastating disorder, Dr. Sacks noticed many aphasics understood what was said to them. In fact, he wrote, "Their friends, their relatives, the nurses who knew them well, could hardly believe, sometimes, that they *were* aphasic. This was because, when addressed naturally, they grasped some or most of the meaning." (Sacks,1970)

If these people were unable to understand the meaning of words, how could they decipher a conversation and respond appropriately? Dr. Sacks concluded it was through extraverbal cues provided by the speakers. These were: "tone of voice, intonation, suggestive emphasis or inflection, as well as all visual cues (one's expressions, personal repertoire and posture)" (Sacks,1970).

Even more interesting, since aphasics are unable to grasp words, Sacks concluded it was impossible to deceive them using words. Aphasics are so proficient at "reading" extraverbal behavior, it is virtually impossible to lie to them. This is because the conscious minds of aphasics are not cluttered with words. Space is opened up for them to consciously evaluate others' nonverbal behavior. They actually enjoy at a conscious level a richness of human communication the rest of us simply process at a deeper, unaware, level.

> *natural speech does not consist of words alone. It consists of utterances—an uttering-forth of one's whole meaning with one's whole being—the understanding of which involves infinitely more than mere word-recognition."*

> Dr. Oliver Sacks,
> *The Man Who Mistook His Wife for a Hat*

Much of Charismatic Communication is transmitted by thousands of minute movements of our bodies. How many times have you received from someone a quick glance that spoke volumes about that person's feelings for you? Chances are, at that moment you had no doubt about whether the person liked or disliked you. But how does a mere look convey clear affection or hatred? How do we judge the difference?

A glance communicating strong meaning requires the flexing and relaxing of different muscles around the eye. It dictates a change in pupil dilation, change of facial muscle tone or color, in the tilt of the head, and so forth. Now, we don't consciously think about all these things and say, "Hey, that's an affectionate look." We process all that information outside conscious awareness. We end up with the feeling of knowing exactly what this person thinks of us.

When we talk with a friend, our senses receive a tremendous amount of information. As we chat, we are not aware that our brains are rapidly processing. Our eyes and ears are powerful receivers, actually collecting all the information within their range. Our eyes see things like change in skin tone or in breathing rate, and tension or relaxation of muscles. Our ears hear things like fluctuation in voice tone or volume, or slight pauses in speech.

Although we have little or no conscious knowledge of it, this information has a strong impact. As information enters the mind, a diversion occurs. A small band enters conscious awareness. This is usually the content of words being said. The remainder funnels back into the unconscious. There it is processed with other information such as the context of the situation, the content of the conversation, and the past history of the individual. Once all this is processed our overall "impression" or "feeling" about the person is formed. This process often requires only fractions of a second.

During the 1988 presidential campaign, when Dan Quayle debated Senator Lloyd Bentsen, Quayle's nonverbal communication lost the battle for him. In actual content, his presentation was similar to Bentsen's. Extraverbally, however, they were miles apart.

Quayle's movements were jerky, his voice strained. His face flushed when he was directly confronted. He had difficulty maintaining eye contact with his opponent, the audience, and the television cameras. His words told us he was a leader. His extraverbal communication said more loudly and clearly that he was not.

Before learning how to create a charismatic or leader-ship presence, it's important to know some of the types of physiological qualities being measured by the unconscious minds of those around you.

POSTURE	Standing straight? Leaning forward or back? Rigid or relaxed? Hunched over or extended? Arms or legs crossed?
MOVEMENTS	Smooth or erratic? Rhythmic or intermittent? Body swaying or motionless?
EYE CONTACT	Constant, rhythmic, or fleeting? Regular or irregular?
SKIN COLOR	Flushed or pale? Even or blotched? How much does it vary?
MUSCLE TONE	Facial muscles relaxed or firm? Taunt or flaccid? Especially important are the jaw muscles and muscles around the eyes.
BREATHING	Where in the chest is breathing: upper, middle, or stomach? Regular or irregular rhythm? Breath held? Sighing?
VOCAL QUALITY	Tonality even? Harsh? Loud or soft? Is tempo fast or slow? Even or erratic? Is volume loud, normal, or soft? Is pitch high, normal, or low? Is it consistent or fluctuating?

Does this seem insignificant? It's not. This is the big stuff. *This is the most important division of information you give to others.* It allows them to make judgments as to just who you are.

People communicate with their whole beings, not just through words. Charismatic communication requires the use of the whole body, not simply words.

BECOMING THE POWER OF YOUR MESSAGE

A major component of Charismatic Communication is *congruence*. In fact, congruence is critical in making charisma work for you. Words may sometimes fail you, but this trait will unerringly pull others toward you.

What is congruence? In its simplest form, congruence means you *truly feel* what the words you use are *saying*. It exists when your physiology, your very person, convey the same information you are speaking. We can see how congruence works even in the simplest transactions of our everyday lives.

What happens if you ask a child to tell the truth and he looks down or away while answering? You don't believe him. Why? Because his verbal and extraverbal behavior don't match. His words are saying, "This is the truth." His body is saying, "I'm lying." The words and the body are incongruent.

When someone smiles with her lips, but her eyes remain coldly flat and there is no light on her face, you don't believe that smile. Why? The smiler's face is incongruent. When a speaker walks slowly up to the podium and says he's happy to be there in a dull, listless voice, who is convinced by those words? No one. Why? The words and the voice are incongruent.

In each of these cases, mixed messages are being sent. And guess what? *People tend to believe extraverbal messages every time*. When you maintain total congruence, you communicate your message 100 percent. That's why others see congruent human beings as believable, strong, and confident. Despite its considerable power, personal congruence is subtle. This has kept it cloaked, its effects unrecognized by most people.

A lack of congruence is endemic. Too few people hold a deep and abiding belief in their positions. Especially in business and political settings, there is a tendency to stand on the most expediential ground. The irony of this is that *congruence thrusts people into a natural leadership position*. Others will naturally gather behind the congruent leader.

Congruence is important because the old adage is true: Our actions *do* speak louder than our words. When you say you will do something and then follow through, you add to your measure of credibility. When you don't, you become not only less believable but also less respected and admired. Remember when President George Bush said, "Read my lips. No new taxes." When taxes were raised, he lost considerable ground with the majority of American people.

In truth, congruent leadership means always following through on what you say, feel, and do. Leadership is not a passive function conducted from behind a desk or a podium. In 1980, Donald Petersen became the CEO of Ford Motor Company. He began talking about "teamwork" and "upward communication." But the company was operating from an entrenched system of restrictive rules and regulations. To attempt change in the very foundation of a corporation's systems is to wage war with the many-tentacled monster called bureaucracy. Words mean little on this battlefield.

Where would you start? Petersen walked into the offices of designers and asked simple questions like: "Do you like these cars?" "Do you feel proud of them?" "Would you park one in your driveway?" (Hillkirk & Jacobson, 1990) When he received negative answers, he told designers to come up with the cars they thought would sell, cars of which they'd be proud.

The results of these first efforts were Ford's 1983 Thunderbird and Ford's incredibly successful Taurus. They became the best selling midsized car in America. That was just the start. During the 1980s, Ford Motor Company turned itself away from the dismal performance of the past decade to make record-breaking profits. In *Fortune* magazine, Petersen was chosen by his fellow CEOs as the nation's most effective leader, surpassing even Lee Iacocca.

Petersen didn't accomplish all this by sitting behind a desk and telling people what he wanted done. He rolled up his shirt sleeves and jumped in. He provided a direction and goal and then participated in making them reality. Petersen was able to lead a company staggering on the edge of failure to a position as a healthy, thriving model of quality and efficiency.

Because all aspects of their being coincide exactly, congruent leaders communicate believability with their very presence. And no matter the circumstances, congruence continues to tell others the truth of our position. Remember seeing Colonel Oliver North during the Iran/Contra hearings? Even after days of intense questioning, all his extraverbal behavior remained congruent. His posture stayed erect. His eyes remained directly fixed on the person to whom he was speaking. His voice seldom changed. In short, his extraverbal actions were congruent with what he said. Result? He was believable.

On his inauguration day, John F. Kennedy sat before millions of television viewers. The ceremony had been delayed. Think of how the pressure builds when there's been a holdup in beginning an important meeting, interview, or speech. Imagine the tension of sitting before television cameras after your inauguration as President of the United States has been delayed.

Yet Kennedy remained relaxed and comfortable. He chatted and smiled with those around him. Everything about him said he was in total control. Viewers didn't have to hear one word he said. His extraverbal behavior made him look like a true leader. In fact, he appeared in such control, newscasters commented that he must have "nerves of steel."

EXERCISE

Think of two people at work who always seem totally congruent. By any chance are they in positions of power?

In both cases, a lot more was transmitted to the unconscious minds of viewers than their conscious minds realized. This is true of any communicative interaction. Our conscious mind focuses on one thing at one time. But our unconscious picks up thousands of pieces of information every second.

When you listen to someone speaking, your conscious mind deals primarily with the verbal message. As you know, this is at best 7 percent of everything being communicated. In contrast, your unconscious mind is easily and quickly making a broad assessment of the speaker's credibility. To judge the level of congruence, the unconscious assesses the similarity or difference between spoken words and extraverbal behavior.

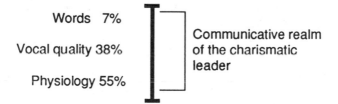

In our own lives, we are tremendously affected by the presence or absence of congruence. How often have you been left confused or unbelieving by something someone told you? There might not have been anything wrong with the words the person spoke. What wasn't right was the way he or she said it.

Even if you couldn't put your finger on why, you were left with the feeling you weren't being told the truth. If you don't already, pay close attention to intuitive feelings. Intuition is not superstition but a sophisticated and complex process. It's an alarm that's set to shrieking by incongruence.

Think about when people communicate with dogs. Because dogs understand the meaning of only a few human words, they depend upon extraverbal behavior in interactions with humans. You can tell a dog it's bad and use hateful words doing so. But, if your tone of voice is loving, the dog will come close, wagging its tail and expecting only affection.

Notice how quickly dogs adapt their behavior when the humans around them change their posture or the expression on their face. If the dog has been socialized, it responds to a smile from its owner by wagging its tail. If the smile continues, the dog will begin to move closer, tail still wagging. If the person changes the expression to a frown, the dog will stop. If the frown continues or deepens, the dog will lie down, back up, or walk away.

As a culture, Americans are word sensitive. Unlike aphasics and animals, most people aren't consciously aware of the messages being conveyed by extraverbal behavior. They overlook the many other ways we all constantly communicate with others. Still, the effects continue to powerfully influence everyone's lives.

If your extraverbal communication does not correspond with the words you speak, you fall into a state of incongruence. Those you wish to lead and influence no longer believe your words. What they do believe is their interpretation of your extraverbal communication. That's when your communication misfires, your effectiveness flounders. You fail.

Think of an interior decorator dealing with a home owner. Suppose the decorator says: "I think this sculpture would make a wonderful addition to your lovely home."

If the decorator's extraverbal behavior did not correspond with the interest and excitement intended in his message, it's as though much of the message was left out. The message getting through would look like this: "I ——— this ——— —— a ——— addition — your ———".

Or worse yet, what is being communicated with the body would actually contradict and confuse the words. The message getting through would look like this: "*I* stupid *this* worried *a* too expensive *addition* won't buy *your* dungeon."

When we communicate information, we often diffuse its effectiveness through a lack of focus and congruence. Even worse, we may communicate the opposite of what we intend. Remember "Stormin" Norman Schwarzkopf during his public press briefings in Operation Desert Storm. What was it that made him such a powerful presence? Simple. The man was incredibly congruent. Every element of his extraverbal communication told us he believed in everything he said. His presence was so powerful no one questioned his abilities.

The simplest way to understand how to achieve congruence is to first understand how incongruence occurs. *For every change in emotional state there is a corresponding change in physiology.* When you allow your thoughts to stray from the subject at hand, your shift in mental focus affects your state of mind. This is marked by a variety of subtle but noticeable changes in your physiology.

For example, what happens when people afraid to speak in front of others are asked to do so? Instead of concentrating on their topic, they create mental pictures of rejection. They begin telling themselves things like "Nobody is really interested," or "You're just making a fool of yourself." In their mind, they see people laughing at or feeling sorry for them.

What about a salesman who, for the fifth time that day, begins his pitch without any conviction? Although he espouses the benefits of his product, inside he is thinking, "They don't want to buy" or "I bet this guy doesn't even have the money for this."

In each case, regardless of what is being said, their "other language" is saying something different. They lack congruence, because what they're saying does not reflect their thoughts. Thoughts, like a typewriter with a fresh ribbon, plainly print out your true feelings all over your body. The message is just waiting to be read by the unconscious minds of others. No matter the words people may use, we develop our own "feelings" about people after "reading" the "printout" of their thoughts.

Suppose, as you talk about a new project during a staff meeting, your thoughts go like this: "If this doesn't fly, I probably won't get my promotion." "What if I overestimated these sales projections?" "I hope I'm not late picking the kids up at school." "Is the boss frowning because he's unhappy with me?"

Each stray thought you have is like a gust of wind blowing your extraverbal communication farther off the course of your intended purpose. As your thoughts change, so do your emotions. This is followed by minute changes in your physiology. You then become less believable. You cannot change the sequence any more than you can make summer follow winter or make old people grow younger.

As a leader, it is vital for you to be sincere in your words and actions throughout your everyday life. Your thoughts *must* correspond with the things you say and do. Only then can the entire package, your very person, create the presence and effect you desire.

To be congruent, thus believable, requires intense mental focus. It doesn't matter if you're selling a product, leading a meeting, or soliciting a donation. Straying thoughts cause people to lose faith in your authority, sincerity, or ability to lead. At best, you look ineffective. At worst, dishonest.

EXERCISE

Next time you're around someone you don't fully trust, make a conscious effort to determine what it is about the person's behavior that makes him or her come across that way.

To understand the importance of congruence, consider actors. To be convincing, they must do more than read lines well. The best of them actually become the character they play. Have you ever heard interviews with great actors where they're asked how they prepared for a part? They often say that weeks or months before, they mapped out every element of the character's behavior, what it was like and how it thought.

Dustin Hoffman in *Rainman*, or Robert DeNiro in *Awakenings* were each convincing in their roles. Why? Because virtually everything in their behavior, down to the smallest detail, created the illusion they were actually the characters they portrayed. The audience was convinced. Could Hoffman and DeNiro control the most minute elements of their physiology? Hardly.

The gift great actors possess is one of tremendous internal focus. They know it isn't enough to memorize lines. To convince the unconscious minds of the audience, there can be no discrepancy between who actors say they are and their extraverbal behavior. This means they must become the other person in their own minds.

They do this by seeing this other person alive in their heads in every detail. Once satisfied with the mental development of the character, they leave themselves, become this other personality. They no longer think of themselves as actors but as the actual characters they're portraying. Because their external behavior is congruent, their roles are believable.

The first and most important way to ensure congruence is to have a direction, a goal about which you feel passionate. When you speak on a subject that excites you and drives your life, congruence is a natural by-product. It is then easy to maintain internal focus, because the subject is part of you. Charismatic leaders embody their causes and goals. They blur the distinction between themselves and the issue for which they stand. They become the personification of the ideal, values, or goals they espouse.

INCREASING YOUR CONGRUENCE	DECREASING YOUR CONGRUENCE
Total focus on your topic or conversation.	Allowing your thoughts to stray.
Speaking about emotionally oriented topics.	Using preplanned gestures, movements, and expressions.
Relaxed body.	Rigid, stiff body.
Low, natural breathing.	High chest, strained breathing.
Well prepared.	Ad-libbing when you're not used to it.
Being flexible to audience needs.	Remaining rigid in thoughts and presentation.

In Short

1. The foundation of charisma lies in the extraverbal realm. Without its mastery, all other skills in this book will fall short of their goals.
2. Charismatic leaders always phrase their plans in optimistic terms.
3. The seemingly magical energy charismatic leaders infuse in their followers originates from their passion. To have charisma, you must be passionate about your goal, leadership, and dream. It all starts there.
4. The strong and directed extraverbal communication charismatic leaders emanate accounts for their powerful presence and grace.
5. It's vital to remember that much of charisma occurs because these leaders communicate with their whole bodies, not just with their words.

3

DEVELOPING THE
TRAITS OF CHARISMA

As with many areas of life, there are specific techniques that allow you to acquire important skills more rapidly than other skills. Though certain human qualities may be the result of personality traits, it doesn't necessarily mean they are beyond the reach of others. It simply means that we must work a little harder to rise to the occasion. This chapter walks you through those catch-up paths to accelerate your capabilities.

THE SOUND OF CHARISMATIC LEADERSHIP

Our Western cultural training causes us to focus primarily on words rather than on the more potent aspects of human communication. That's why people who attempt to inspire, motivate, or arouse the best in others often fail. Most people don't recognize the sometimes simple factors that make all the difference in creating consistent success. For example, despite an overconcern with the *words* they speak, they never consider how their *voice* increases or lessens their ability to affect others. Yet, *the quality of your voice can impact others as much as five times more powerfully than do the words you say.*

This is why most people don't come close to using their voices optimally. They lack vocal personality. Their voices lack the distinctive individual qualities that confer emotion and power on everyday speech. This is unfortunate, because people with vocal personality are able to deliver more powerful and effective messages. This is even more so when it is contrasted with the deadpan, monotone voices all too common in our society.

What about you? Does your voice assist you in being your best or does it sabotage you? Do you have a vocal personality that portrays leadership and confidence? Does it put people at ease, make you sound friendly and approachable? Or do you come across as weak, uncertain, dull, cold, uncaring?

The untrained voice can be a great liability to one's leadership effectiveness. The personality characteristics people can attribute to certain types of voices may be far different from those we believe we're portraying.

Personality Perceptions Created Through Vocal Quality

Vocal Quality	Perceptions Created
Flat	Lacking in enthusiasm, drive, ambition or ability. Unemotional, laziness, or boredom can also be communicated.
Nasally	Weak; lacking in leadership ability. A follower; one without a strong personality. Whiner.
Throaty	Careful, overly cautious or timid. Holding back one's thoughts, emotions, or ideas. Unable to express one's self.

Loud	Arrogant, insensitive, brash. A bully or one lacking in social graces. One filled with him or herself.
Lite	Young, immature and childish. This person could also be perceived as mentally unstable or dishonest.
Resonate	Powerful, directed, and confident. Being comfortable with one's self and one's environment. Polished, smooth, graceful.

Your voice has much to do with how others perceive you and your ability to be charismatic. You need a strong, resonant, colorful voice full of emotion. It can support and carry your words in a dynamic fashion. Rather than detracting from it, this voice enhances your personality and makes it unique. Think about fully dressed voices like those of Winston Churchill, Martin Luther King, Jr., John F. Kennedy, or Oprah Winfrey, Richard Burton, and Walter Cronkite.

Two elements are most important to a strong vocal personality. They are proper breathing and being emotionally expressive. Whole books have been written, classes given, on developing your voice. We couldn't hope to cover it all in one section or even in one chapter. Following is a short course on developing a strong vocal personality. If you need further help in developing yours, consult one of the many fine books on the subject.

EMOTIONAL EXPRESSIVENESS

As you remember from Chapter 1, the use of emotion is a vital element of charisma. Still, we are often taught to use a "poker face" during business interactions. The perfect companion for the "poker face" is the "poker voice"—the vocal equivalent of a blank face. In work settings, we often attempt to create that "professional air" by reducing the emotions we express. This form of communication does little to enhance leadership standing. It also makes those around you uncomfortable.

In contrast, charismatic leaders infuse strong and productive emotions in others by first displaying them themselves. They have the courage to express without hesitation their feelings about issues and subjects. While others sit becalmed, worrying about rejection, charismatic leaders sail ahead. They weave an emotional net capable of capturing everyone in its wake.

Charismatic leaders not only possess full, resonant voices but have an emotionally charged voice. Their voices always display a wide range of emotions. Whatever the message calls for—sadness, love, anger, joy, boredom, surprise—charismatic leaders sound like the emotion they are expressing.

Think about the variety of emotionally driven voices each of us uses in different contexts. Besides our work voice, we have a sensual voice, a parental voice, and so on. We naturally switch to these voices without thinking about it. As we step into a certain role we just assume the voice quality that goes with it.

Think about a time you discussed business with someone in his or her office and a close friend, spouse, or child called the person on the telephone. It's the rare person who responds in the same voice used to talk business with you. And when the conversation was over, the person most likely hung up the receiver and resumed the "business voice" without skipping a beat.

Most people feel their voices always indicate the emotions of which they speak. Very often they do not. More often, others are reading our emotional state from our facial expressions. By missing this element of the communication process we reduce our impact on others. We also appear incongruent, not believable.

EXERCISE

This is a good exercise for developing the emotional impact of your voice. It will also become a foundation exercise for future development.

Using the "Ahhhhh" sound, express the following emotions in your voice:

Delight	Determination
Sadness	Doubt
Surprise	Boredom
Sympathy	Fear
Joy	Disgruntled
Interest	Ecstasy

UNLEASHING THE POWER OF YOUR NATURAL VOICE

It may be surprising to some, but breathing is the secret to having a unique, dynamic vocal personality. In fact, *you can unleash the powerful voice given to you at birth simply by using your chest, abdomen, and throat correctly.*

Many people breathe high in their chests and rely on short, rapid breaths. This places too much dependence on throat muscles. It substantially hinders the resonance, color, and power of your voice. Stress and tension in shoulders, neck, and chest results in a high-pitched, squeaky voice. Michael Jackson, Dr. Ruth Westheimer, PeeWee Herman, and Mike Tyson are examples. A voice such as this commands little authority and in many cases seems comical.

A fitting voice comes initially from a relaxed body. Relaxing the muscles in your shoulders, neck, and chest allows the air from your lungs to boldly flow unobstructed through your throat and vocal cords. It deepens and brings resonance to your voice.

EXERCISE

The easiest way to bring back your natural voice is to be relaxed. If at any time you find yourself becoming stressed, try this simple exercise.

1. Breathing through your mouth, take in a deep 3-second breath.
2. Hold the breath for 3 seconds.
3. Exhale completely and don't breathe in for 3 seconds.
4. Most people repeat this process 3 or 4 times, then just begin breathing normally again. This is especially useful just before stepping up to the podium for a speech.

When you were an infant you had perfect breathing. It involved most of your body and centered around your abdomen. Unfortunately, as we grow up we unconsciously pick up bad habits from those around us and through life's experiences.

If you had a parent who remained keyed-up and tense, you picked up those habits. You tend to breathe rapidly and high in the chest just as he or she did. You tighten your neck muscles and speak through your throat. Or maybe you had a parent with a listless voice. It expressed no emotion, had no energy. Words were just carelessly dropped out to deliver a lackluster message whenever it was necessary. All children are natural little sponges soaking up what occurs around them. So we adopt a voice we come to believe is ours.

Or maybe as a child you consciously developed what you thought would be a more appropriate voice. At some point, you may have been teased by other children about the way your voice sounded. You vowed it wouldn't sound that way again. Your solution was to tighten your throat and change the way you breathed. It quickly became habit.

Whatever the reason, for many of us the voice we are speaking with isn't really ours. The next step in bringing out your *true* vocal personality is to begin breathing correctly once again. The appropriate breath supporting a powerful, resonant voice fills the belly, not the chest. High chest breaths encourage a high-pitched, thin voice. A breath taken low in the belly supports a strong flow of air through a relaxed field of vocal cords. It creates the full resonance prized by professional speakers and those in public life.

EXERCISE

A good way to begin developing resonance in your voice is to follow this exercise 4 to 5 times per week. The key is to breathe into your low belly rather than from your upper chest. This type of breath is effective because a large amount of air can be slowly released without putting strain on the vocal cords. With a little practice it can be done quite naturally and slowly.

1. Take in a 3-second breath through your mouth that fills your belly.
2. Sitting straight, lift your head slightly higher than normal and open your mouth.
3. Say "Ahhhhh" while exhaling for 6 to 8 seconds. Keep your throat wide open. Your voice should be deep and low.
4. When you feel a deep vibration in your chest you will know that you're developing a rich resonance. Note: There should be no strain whatsoever on your vocal cords, as correct speech creates little strain on the body. Should you feel any discomfort consult a speech therapist.

THE PRESENCE OF CHARISMATIC LEADERSHIP

It is vitally important to fully prepare your mind and body for a meeting, presentation, speech, or conversation. This means more than knowing what to say. It means preprogramming your mind to direct all your action. You must precisely define what your thoughts, mannerisms, and actions are to be and imprint them on your mind. There are two good ways to do this. The first is to become more attached to your emotions, and the second involves much the same type of preprogramming process actors use.

The Extraverbal Techniques of Power

Many Westerners have learned to suppress their emotions through a variety of means. It's considered bad form, particularly in the business setting, to have emotions seen by others. This is viewed as somehow detrimental to us.

Yet, one of the reasons the world's great charismatic leaders were so beloved was because of the level of emotion they showed. They were not stoic and rigid but warm, approachable people. Despite their mammoth popularity and power, we watched as they were moved emotionally by the same things we all are. We loved them for it.

People all share the same human emotions. But most people don't allow themselves to appropriately display their feelings through their bodies and voices. You'd be hard pressed to find a bigger, burlier, and more decisive military leader than General Norman Schwarzkopf. Yet, when he began to discuss American casualties in the Persian Gulf war, his eyes welled with tears and his voice broke. He showed that despite his powerful position, he still had the feelings and compassion of a loving person.

To be effective, you must be sure your body sends the same messages as your words do. You need to master at least one of two techniques for doing this. An effective technique for ensuring congruence and communicating emotions is to reexperience the emotions while speaking. Unfortunately, most of us were taught to communicate in business settings by concentrating on the words of a script. *When we focus on words rather than on the experiences the words describe, we become detached from their emotional content.* We become as interesting as a statistician reciting numbers.

Relating a series of words does nothing to activate your body and voice. To do that, you must actually relive the experience in your mind. This is far more powerful, because you are describing what you are actually seeing, hearing, and feeling in your head. As you fully relive the experience, you move into the desired emotional state. In the desired state, every nuance of your behavior—from tone of voice to facial expressions—acts as a guide to those watching and listening. Your extraverbal behavior actually teaches others how to act and feel about what you're saying.

Don't ever memorize a script. Instead, prepare by re-playing over and over in your mind the experiences you'll be relating. Make them as vivid as possible. Suppose you're going to be relating a number of stories during a sales-training session. Firmly implant in your mind each of those stories. "Film" them as though they were movies you were going to play on the screen of your mind. Each time you tell the story you will be fresh, sincere, and congruent. Of course, you will never relate the story exactly the same way twice. That's fine. Sincerity is far more valuable to a charismatic leader than consistency of wording.

People who memorize scripts almost always come across as insincere and manipulative when attempting to elicit emotions in others. Most often their heads jut out toward those to whom they are speaking, their eyes widen, and their eyebrows raise up. They appear to be pushing words out rather than sharing an experience.

On the other hand, you can always tell when someone is relating a story he or she has actually experienced. Normally, the head will move back and the eyes defocus, because the person is focusing on internal imagery. The speech will be fluid and consistent with the type of experience. Although seemingly subtle, the unconscious minds of listeners pick up on these nuances. Should your total behavior not completely match your words, should you not be congruent, you will not have a charismatic impact no matter what else you may do.

One reason for this has been suggested by a number of researchers. When you memorize verbatim speeches, sales scripts, or presentation, you are accessing only the left side of your brain. This side deals with linear thinking, words, and logic. The problem is that this side of your brain tends to miss the emotional elements of the message. By concentrating simply on the words, you lose their deeper meaning because their emotional importance is stored in the right side of the brain.

It takes a coordinated effort from both sides of our brain to achieve the graceful strength of charisma. When concentrating solely on left-brain accessing, a sort of asymmetry occurs in our movement. We are attempting to "logically" induce emotion or importance into our message. The contradiction shows. We look insincere, our gestures seem contorted, uncomfortable. We cannot appear dynamic or powerful.

A wonderful example of how this level of mental accessing can create congruence can be seem in the Public Broadcasting System's television series, "The Power of Myth." It features journalist Bill Moyers and reknowned mythologist Joseph Campbell. Moyers leads Campbell through a wonderful dialogue on the impact of mythology on human history and development.

This subject matter has the potential to be dry as a desert river bed. But Campbell's constant use of word pictures and stories instead creates a flood of emotion. Even veteran interviewer Bill Moyers is visibly struck by Campbell's ability to create a vivid and precise mosaic without ever missing a beat.

Campbell's strategy for charismatically holding an audience spellbound for hours is easy to see. When he speaks of the passion of an ancient culture he, too, becomes passionate. When he talks of destruction, love, envy, or fear his whole person speaks along with him. The series, available on video, is worth viewing.

Notice how Campbell's head is relaxed and set back as he speaks. His eyes are defocused. His hands reach out and seemingly touch some unseen screen on which a brilliant variety of movies play. He uses no notes when discussing his complex topic. He just talks about the scene playing in his head. He makes you see, hear, and feel it along with him.

Elegant and graceful total communication (verbal and extraverbal) is a product of a solid knowledge of your subject and an emotional spontaneity. Instead of relying on scripts, great leaders use clusters of memories, images, and ideas. These provide a general guideline of thoughts. Memorizing only small groupings of words and phrases continually activates both sides of the brain. This releases a constant flow of words on demand. It all comes together in a powerful, congruent message throughout your body.

Another method that's often used to develop personal congruence is the kind of preprogramming process often used by actors. It will help keep you congruent in all decision making as you move toward realizing your greater vision.

During World War II, General George Patton was asked by a news reporter how he could make immediate decisions committing troops to situations where, if his decision were wrong, thousands of American lives could be lost. Patton said there was nothing his enemy could do that he had not already gone over and over in his mind. He thought of every possible move and strategy that could be made and used. No decision he ever made in battle was hasty. Each had already been gone over in his mind time and time again.

You can use the following process to preprogram your speech, meeting, or presentation. *Remember: For it to be effective, you must repeat it entirely over and over:*

1. Once you have practiced your presentation successfully a number of times, find a place where you are alone. See yourself on stage, in the board room, and so forth, giving your presentation the way you want it to be. Begin by seeing your face, slowly expanding your vision to include your entire body. Notice the directedness of every movement, the passion, the total expression exhibited in every part of your body.

Now, turn on the sound. Listen to your voice. Adjust it until you sound as though you have reached complete comfort with the audience. Regulate your vocal tone and volume so your voice controls and captivates the room. Hear the fluidity and consistency of your message.

Next, expand your vision to include the entire room. Envision your audience spellbound, sitting on the edge of their seats. Notice the looks of interest and understanding on their faces. Listen to the laughter you've elicited from them, their questions.

2. Now find yourself actually up and on the stage. Feel the heat of the lights. See your audience before you, hear their laughter. Let yourself become aware of all the strong and wonderful feelings that envelop you as you elegantly command your listeners. Let that feeling grow.

As you continue your presentation, walk down through the audience. Now see their faces up close, feel their enjoyment. Notice the way you move as you command your audience. Feel the words flowing from your throat. Feel the rhythm created in the room by your words and movements. Make broad gestures and talk to individuals in your audience. Run through the entire presentation thoroughly in your mind.

3. After you have been through the entire presentation a few times, begin to create problem scenarios. Work through them as gracefully as you first delivered your speech. Give yourself a heckler or two. Run through your presentation with a disinterested audience, have a slide projector that doesn't work, or come up with a missing chalkboard. How do you handle these situations? Work out ways to easily and elegantly handle each of these situations. Come up with as many difficult scenarios as you can and develop at least one method for getting out of each of them.

Most charismatic communicators go through such steps literally hundreds of times before speaking to an audience. The process does a number of things. *You will be far more relaxed during the actual presentation, feeling as though you've spoken to this audience many times before.* Like General Patton, no matter what problem arises you will handle it easily. That's because you will have dealt with many more difficult ones time and again in your mind.

You will have given your mind a blueprint for the presentation and conditioned it through repetition. *You will also be able to speak with continuity without using notes.* Your mind will have the information so embedded in it that notes will be not only completely unnecessary but would actually slow you down.

Using the techniques of great actors to preprogram and immerse yourself in your capability, you will generate wonderful congruence throughout any type of leadership interaction. *This technique puts you in control of your abilities and actions rather than leaving them to chance.* Vivid repetitions will condition a precise set of behaviors. You will then embody and deliver your message in a way that excites and motivates your audience.

THE CHARISMA TEST

This book is directed toward one goal: to provide you with the tools of Charismatic Communication. Whether we realize it or not, each of us is charismatic at certain times in our lives. That's because the ability to connect with and emotionally affect others (the essence of charisma) is a part of being human. Still, we haven't known specifically what charisma was and how we could use it to benefit everyone involved. Therefore, we were unable to consistently inspire the best efforts of others.

There is a lot of information in the pages of this book. Each element is equally important in the development of your personal charisma. We found, however, that it often works best if you initially place more focus on certain techniques and skills. Which those are for you depend upon your current communication emphasis and perceptual focus.

We have designed this simple and painless test to help you better direct your efforts at quickly attaining a powerful level of charisma.

THE TEST

Move through this test quickly. Don't agonize. Make a check mark behind the answer that first jumps into mind and move on. There is no "pass" or "fail."

1. Which is most important?

    A. Procedures ___

    B. Negotiating ___

    C. Conversation ___

2. How do you prefer to receive directions at work?

    A. In a team or group meeting ___

    B. In written form ___

    C. In a one-on-one meeting with your supervisor ___

3. Which is most comfortable for you?

    A. Solid facts ___

    B. Relationships ___

    C. Flexibility ___

4. Which is best?

    A. The actual ___

    B. The possible ___

    C. The consistent ___

5. Which is the best leadership philosophy?

    A. Commitment to people ___

    B. Commitment to organizations ___

    C. Commitment to goals ___

6. What is the most effective utilization of human resources?

    A. Assign tasks according to knowledge of the people ___

B. Assign tasks according to current needs of the organization ___

C. Assign tasks that allow individuals to grow ___

7. As a manager or leader are you more

    A. Bold ___

    B. Thorough ___

    C. Clever ___

8. Others most need

    A. Direction ___

    B. Motivation ___

    C. Team work ___

9. Which is most important for leadership?

    A. Enthusiasm ___

    B. Cooperation ___

    C. Ability to administer ___

10. People do their best work when they are

    A. Consolidated toward one goal ___

    B. Grouped into task-oriented teams ___

    C. Driven for personal reasons ___

11. Would you prefer to

    A. Talk to people ___

    B. Encourage people ___

    C. Administer people ___

12. When communicating one should be

    A. Spontaneous ___

    B. Literal ___

    C. Technical ___

13. People respond best to

    A. Procedures ___

    B. Aspiration ___

    C. Affiliation ___

14. Leadership is a by-product of
    A. Inspiration ___
    B. Influence ___
    C. Status ___

15. The most important leadership quality is to
    A. Have a vision ___
    B. Be able to motivate ___
    C. Possess a strong technical background ___

16. Which is the safest stance to take?
    A. Pessimistic ___
    B. Optimistic ___
    C. Neutral ___

17. Which is most important during a conversation?
    A. That they understand your point ___
    B. That they leave with positive thoughts ___
    C. That you've had the opportunity to say your piece ___

18. People normally
    A. Want to do their best ___
    B. Need guidance ___
    C. Want affiliation ___

19. Publicly correcting an employee can
    A. Never be useful ___
    B. Sometimes be useful ___
    C. Always be useful ___

20. Which would be the most fulfilling professional challenge?
    A. Turning around a failing company ___
    B. Stabilizing a wildly fluctuating company ___
    C. Rekindling a demoralized sales staff ___

21. Which is the most mysterious leadership concept?
    A. Why others can't get people to take action ___
    B. Getting people to take action ___
    C. Getting people to want to take action ___

22. When a problem arises do you
    A. Look for ways to minimize its impact ___
    B. Look for the other problems it will create ___
    C. Look for the ways it benefits your organization ___

23. Among your colleagues are you
    A. Popular ___
    B. One of the team ___
    C. Respected ___

24. As a manager or leader do you show appreciation to your employees by
    A. Seeking out and acknowledging their accomplishments ___
    B. Letting them know their work speaks for itself ___
    C. Complimenting them when you happen to see accomplishments ___

25. People are more
    A. Static
    B. Flexible
    C. Dynamic

Scoring Your Test

Once you have completed the test, check your answers with the following scoring key. Each answer is worth one, two, or three points. Once you have written in your points for each answer, total your score at the bottom. This number will enable you to determine where your natural aptitudes lie. This will guide you toward the chapters of this book that will initially be most beneficial to your success.

Question	Points	Your Score
1. A	1	
B	2	
C	3	_____
2. A	3	
B	1	
C	2	_____
3. A	1	
B	3	
C	2	_____
4. A	2	
B	3	
C	1	_____
5. A	3	
B	1	
C	2	_____
6. A	2	
B	3	
C	1	_____
7. A	3	
B	1	
C	2	_____
8. A	1	
B	3	
C	2	_____
9. A	3	
B	2	
C	1	_____

10. A   1
    B   2
    C   3   _____

11. A   2
    B   3
    C   1   _____

12. A   3
    B   2
    C   1   _____

13. A   1
    B   3
    C   2   _____

14. A   3
    B   2
    C   1   _____

15. A   2
    B   3
    C   1   _____

16. A   1
    B   3
    C   2   _____

17. A   1
    B   3
    C   2   _____

18. A   3
    B   1
    C   2   _____

19. A   3
    B   2
    C   1   _____

20.	A	2	
	B	1	
	C	3	_____
21.	A	3	
	B	1	
	C	2	_____
22.	A	2	
	B	1	
	C	3	_____
23.	A	3	
	B	1	
	C	2	_____
24.	A	3	
	B	1	
	C	2	_____
25.	A	1	
	B	2	
	C	3	_____

YOUR TOTAL _____

25	50	75
Bureaucratic/ Technical	Manager/ Leader	Charismatic Leader

Where You Stand

Bureaucratic/Technical 25– 41

Those who achieve scores within this range are usually more comfortable with the complexities of numbers, systems, statistics, and technology. They tend to be more process oriented rather than people oriented. They may be good at conceptualizing the overall needs of an organization or placing intense mental focus on a small, intricate problem. When weighing decisions, they place the greatest weight on logic and fact.

Often they are intellectually oriented managers and leaders who are well schooled in their professional area of expertise. Because they maintain the bulk of their focus on the structure of things, they tend to overlook constantly fluctuating interactions of people. This means they can find the concept of Charismatic Communication difficult to grasp.

If you scored within this category, you will do best to begin your training by creating strong bonds with those with whom you constantly interact. Chapters 4 and 5 focus on the behavioral strategies used by great charismatic leaders to create strong and lasting bonds with those they lead.

Manager/Leader 42– 58

Those achieving scores within this range most often fall within the Western definition of the model manager or leader. These people tend to strike more of a balance between the technical and their concerns for individuals. They are able to see the broad picture and know where to go with it.

They are very much concerned with reality and tend to focus on the here and now. Because of this, abstractions and theory are of little use to them, playing a small role in their thinking. They are often the negotiators, the trouble shooters, the diplomats of the business world. It is these manager/leaders who provide the mainstay of Western business practices.

These individuals often naturally use tools of influence and persuasion when leading. They may even be charismatic from time to time. However, their concern for workers can be a source of frustration to them. This is because the management/leadership tools with which they have been provided do not allow them to consistently motivate others to action.

Much of this book will make immediate sense to those in this group. If you scored within this range, however, the information in Chapters 2 and 3 will best serve you initially. It deals with your ability to motivate others using extraverbal behavior. It will allow you to drop the old business deadpan face and enable you to energize your already established leadership skills.

Charismatic Leader 59– 75

Those scoring in the mid fifties and up are those most likely to have considerable natural charismatic qualities. They look toward the interactions of people and consider others' reactions to daily life. When dealing with people, charismatic leaders are concerned with the kinds of responses they are getting from people rather than with the content of the conversation.

Rather than flooding people's minds with all the data and information necessary to understand an entire project, they prefer to motivate with an idea today. They feel they can always realign the efforts of others tomorrow if it becomes necessary.

Charismatic leaders effectively manage the emotions of people. They are the ones best equipped to get the best from others. They realize to be effective they must have a solid grounding in technical, managerial, and leadership skills. Yet they also take the next step, the use of Charismatic Communication.

These people lead others by infusing their own excitement, enthusiasm, and power into those around them using a defined communicative code. They always place the emotional will and energy of those they lead at the top of their responsibility list. This is a task easy to perform once understood.

If you fall comfortably within this category, place your emphasis on Chapters 7, 8, and 10. Chapter 7 deals with the foundation of inspiration. Chapter 8 deals with a variety of techniques for inspiring others, while Chapter 10 demonstrates the use of Charismatic Communication in a variety of settings. These will enhance your personal leadership and communication abilities greatly.

In Short

1. Your voice communicates your natural leadership presence as much as five times more powerfully than what you say. If you want a powerful leadership presence you must develop a powerful, graceful voice.
2. We live in a culture where, for the most part, we are suppose to suppress our emotions and feelings. The powerful presence of charismatic leaders, however, comes from their ability to communicate the emotions of their message through extraverbal channels.
3. Probably the best method for communicating your message and leadership fully (both at the logical and emotional levels) is to have an intense mental focus on your subject matter as you're speaking about it. Stray thoughts communicate weakness at the extraverbal level.

THE CHARISMA FACTOR

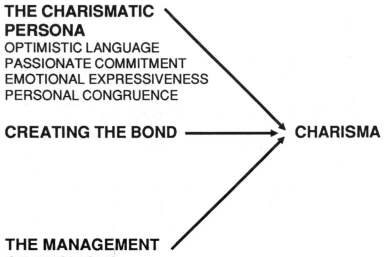

THE CHARISMATIC PERSONA
OPTIMISTIC LANGUAGE
PASSIONATE COMMITMENT
EMOTIONAL EXPRESSIVENESS
PERSONAL CONGRUENCE

CREATING THE BOND → **CHARISMA**

THE MANAGEMENT OF EMOTIONS

From Likability to Leadership

4

THE BEST-KEPT SECRET OF THE WORLD'S GREAT LEADERS

Charismatic leaders are masters at getting the job done. They share a common vision with their followers, easily drawing the best efforts from others. Their endeavors prosper as people enthusiastically apply individual talents and energies. Everyone around them is vested in success. Impressive things are accomplished out of mutual liking, respect, and trust. It's no wonder these leaders enjoy the steadfast loyalty of their followers.

Charismatic leaders do not depend on the kindness of fate nor on the whim of elements outside themselves. They have energy enough to fuel the air about them. None of their energy is dissipated by struggles to gain and maintain leadership. We have all seen these leaders. Yet leaders with charisma create environments where employees thrive, clients enthusiastically purchase, or donors happily support a cause. And we have wondered, how do they do it?

The first step for any charismatic leader must be the creation of a bond that causes others to eagerly accept their ideas and leadership. In this chapter we look at the fascinating phenomenon called entrainment used by charismatic leaders to generate natural acceptance with others. In fact, it appears to be the glue that bonds people, groups, and entire societies together all over the world.

WHY PEOPLE WILL FOLLOW YOUR LEADERSHIP

Think about the early stages of any endeavor or project. There is a familiar jockeying for the leadership position. Even when a person is designated leader, there may be subtle or overt challenges. Then there are those who find themselves leader in name only. They stand in front of the group, knowing in their heart that real leadership is coming from someone sitting before them.

Most people willingly relinquish their own possibilities for leadership. They don't want any part of this leading stuff. It's too risky, too much trouble, just not worth it. Whatever reason they voice to themselves or others, there is a common motive lurking below the surface. *People choose not to lead because they are afraid: afraid of being inadequate, afraid of accepting responsibility, afraid of being rejected.* Most of all, *they fear failure*, with its potential loss of respect, status, or position.

So what, you say. Who cares why people don't want to lead—just so long as they stay out of my way. You should care for two reasons. One, your ultimate success remains dependent on these people. And, two, *the very factors that cause people to relinquish leadership can make them ineffective or dangerous followers.* Like shifting sand, their fear provides an unsound foundation upon which to build your leadership.

Fear as a motivator too often results in marginal efforts producing marginal results. Practically speaking, *people following out of fear are seldom the exceptional helpers great leaders need.* These people will do enough to stay out of trouble but not much more. They are not risk takers but experts at just getting by.

There's another problem with fear-motivated followers. Their first loyalty is to safety rather than to you or the project. How much time do you want to spend watching your back? The truth is, *those motivated by fear can quickly turn against you.* Feel quiet pity for leaders who must keep an eye on the "fear barometer," constantly checking for changes that affect their success. These leaders are susceptible in another way. They're always in danger of having their leadership usurped by someone carrying a bigger club. It's this kind of leadership that causes us to say, "It's just not worth it."

Then how *do* leaders ensure the efforts and loyalty of others? Charismatic leaders begin by transcending conventional techniques and ploys based on fear or manipulation. Using a distinct process, *they create at a deep level a connection so strong it inspires others to willingly gather around them.* Sharing the vision and the promise, they welcome others to the journey.

There is an exquisite sense of timing involved. Charismatic leaders know when people feel comfortable enough to accept their leadership without confrontation or question. They watch for the explicit cues that say, "Now." From this point on, people follow them. They follow, not because they are afraid or feel they have to, but because it is what they *want* to do.

THE FOUR LEVELS OF LEADERSHIP CONNECTION

To have a consistent following there must be a connection between the leader and those being led. There are four different types of leadership connections into which people can enter:

Rapport
Binding
Control
Entrainment

Since the early 1980s a great deal has been discussed and written about rapport. There's no doubt that rapport creates an acceptable level of comfort or a feeling of ease between people. Using rapport in business transactions is already popular among certain groups and businesses because it is a handy tool for easing human interaction and because it's an easy connection to make. However, *rapport building techniques create a link far too weak for creating that charismatic effect.* It's nice when people have a comfortable interaction. But there's nothing in it that will cause one to eagerly follow the other.

Rapport-building techniques consist mainly of matching things like the other's behavior, attitudes, or beliefs. We all go through similar natural movements virtually every day. These techniques simply refine our natural activity into a formalized process.

Think about two people meeting for the first time. Usually they begin to search for common ground. They talk to each other, most often beginning with questions.

"What do you do?"

"How long have you been with the company?"

"What college did you go to?"

"What's your favorite place to eat around here?"

Establishing commonality is useful. By itself, however, it won't establish undying support. Rapport techniques are really like the spices you add to a main dish. A little rapport added to the entrainment process used by charismatic leaders enhances it and contributes to a satisfying result. But, that doesn't mean that rapport substitutes for entrainment any more than a handful of spice would be an adequate main course.

Another type of leadership is called binding. While binding will bring people together, it is a restriction-based connection. In legal terminology, "to bind over" means "oblige by bond to appear at a court." This type of human connection uses a bond to create a sense of obligation out of which others act. There is not a healthy drawing forth of followers' best efforts. Instead, there's an attempt to secure their support by calling upon sense of duty, fear of authority, need for safety, or awe of moral force.

A binding connection is strong but appeals to limits rather than to strengths. Thus, it works well only with the more dependent. It can be seen in action in any co-dependent situation. The problem is, stronger, more powerful people (the kind you most want at your side) fight against it. You find yourself doing battle with your own warriors.

Binding connection usually transcends logic or reason. Those in a binding connection seldom seek verification of what the leader says. Their desire to serve overcomes and quiets the inquiring part of their minds. You need the special insights, talents, and abilities of those around you, including their questioning. So, while binding is not inherently bad, it isn't the best for truly effective leadership. Also, it can easily be abused and lends itself to exploitation.

You can tell when people have bound themselves to another. They will overtly protect and stand up for that person, no matter the circumstances. *Any* disagreement with or criticism of a leader will be met with deep resentment and anger by bound members of a group. Binding is most often created by prolonged exposure to an emotionally manipulative person or through the use of covert hypnotic techniques.

A third type of leadership is control. Control oriented leaders are strongly and clearly manipulative. Victims under control lose the desire and ability to individually live their lives. Individuality is replaced with a desire only to please and serve the specific person or organization. This is readily seen in cult leaders.

Command is gained over the susceptible through the use of specific and powerful techniques. These are usually applied over a prolonged period of time. Some of the more common methods to gain control are prolonged exposure to covert hypnotic techniques, physical and sensory deprivation, values and belief eradication and substitution techniques.

The type of connection, however, that charismatic leaders create is called *entrainment*. Not only is entrainment respectful of freedom of thought and personal control, it creates a stimulating bond of trust also known as the "Lik-

---

THE FOUR TYPES OF LEADERSHIP CONNECTION

Level of Connection	Techniques to Achieve
Rapport	Physical matching and mirroring.
Binding	Prolonged exposure to entrainment or covert hypnotic techniques.
Control	Prolonged exposure to covert hypnotic techniques or values/belief-eradication techniques.
Entrainment (The Realm of Charismatic Leaders)	Rhythmic Matching and Synchrony.

---

ability Factor." *This naturally occurring phenomenon is at the heart of every charismatic leader's success.* When it occurs, *the neurology of one person literally connects to and drives the neurology of another.* There are a variety of techniques used to synchronize one's behavior with that of another to create entrainment. Every major charismatic leader studied in our research consistently used one or more of these techniques. In this chapter, you will learn exactly what entrainment is and why it works.

ENSURING YOUR POSITION AS THE LEADER

We all naturally seek connection to others. It's a basic part of our humanness and social structure. We all experience and observe the ties connecting co-workers, spouses, parents and their child, or members of a team. What is it that is driving us to link up with others?

As social animals we have always lived in packs. Throughout our history as a species, our very survival has depended upon banding together and working toward the common good.

> *"For the humanoids to survive their early years on the exposed plains, they must have depended upon having close-knit social groups, compensating for their vulnerability by being alert and organized." Also, ". . . Because humanoids could not outrun other dangerous animals, they had to become more socially organized to defend themselves from leopards and hyenas." (McCrone, 1991)*

Any survival-based trait remains a powerful part of our humanness. There are few stronger than our need to be connected with others. Given time, even hostages will often create a bond with one or more of the captors who took their freedom. The bond can become so strong that hostages will actually protect captors during a rescue operation, a phenomenon known as the Stockholm syndrome.

Colonel Charlie Beckwith, the head of the DELTA counterterrorism team, expressed his concern about this while briefing President Jimmy Carter on the Iranian hostage-rescue plan. In his book *Delta Force* Beckwith recounts telling the president: "There is no way of knowing how they [the hostages] will behave. Will they try to protect their guards? That's a syndrome common to situations where hostages have been held a long time."

Bonding occurs everyday in a positive way as well. We feel comfortable with members of sports teams, our churches, co-workers, friends, loved ones, and leaders. We are drawn tightly to these people through some unexplained bonding process. Yet, this "process" is the foundation of our social fabric, relationships, team efforts, and indeed the charismatic leaders' ability to inspire.

That's why charismatic leaders ensure their leadership when they establish basic human connection with their followers. The bond they create is composed of a set of feelings linked one to the other. The resulting tie is more powerful than any chain. *Once connected, others naturally accept a leader.* This profound bond is what we call entrainment.

Once you establish entrainment, people are far more *willing* to follow your leadership. Because they are connected to you at such a fundamental level, *they are naturally drawn to your leadership.* They give careful consideration to what you say, are eager for a part in your viable endeavors.

Another benefit of connection is that it naturally results in a feeling of liking. This is important. Leadership is often made more difficult than it needs to be. When people don't feel they really know or like someone, they are far more skeptical. But, when they do like someone there's a different outlook on his or her ideas and leadership.

Sometimes followers spend an inordinate amount of time analyzing and examining what you say and do. They judge you by a far stricter scale, are more critical and harsher than they need to be. Once entrained, however, these same people feel comfortable. That comfort creates liking. You may then circumvent stumbling blocks that otherwise would trip you, causing you to stumble.

As our unconscious minds monitor and search the environment for others with whom to connect, *it uses similarity as its primary criterion.* It then moves us toward and unconsciously connects us to the people who make us feel good. If you want people to have these feelings toward you, *they must perceive you as similar to them in some way.* It all begins with that.

The more similar to us people are, the more we inherently accept, trust, and respect them. And the more like us someone is, the easier it is to understand him or her. We have a strong need to understand everything and everyone. It has always been vital for us to comprehend and use to our advantage the circumstances in which we found ourselves. "Adapt or perish," was a basic tenet in the law of survival. Today, our physical lives are no longer at stake, but our success most certainly is. That's why our unconscious mind continually strives to understand.

When we understand people because they are like us we can trust them to behave in specific, predictable ways. To understand how basic and important this is, imagine that a conference table you often find yourself seated at is a roaring camp fire in a primitive clearing. Now, dress the men and women who normally sit around that table with you in pieces of skins and furs. Look out into the dark beyond the dancing light of the fire. The adversary out there isn't a competing company. It's a pack of growling animals intent on tearing the flesh from your bones. Do you want to fight that pack alone? More important, could you fight that pack alone and win? No, you don't and you couldn't. *In order to win, you need others beside you as cunning and willing to fight as you.* They are the ones you can depend on, because *they are the same as you.*

This creates an interesting dynamic. *The more similar people are to us, the easier it is to understand them. The easier it is to understand them, the better we feel around them. The better we feel around them, the more we want to maintain contact with them.*

When you cause people to feel good, you utilize another natural human inclination: the drive to seek pleasure and avoid pain. While doing anything they can to avoid people or situations that cause them pain, *humans constantly search for positive feelings.* They will go back again and again to the source of pleasure, even if there is no logical reason for it.

Entrainment generates compatibility, rapport, and trust, feelings that cause humans to feel good. So, we naturally feel good around those with whom we have entrained. Because people like you and want to be around you, they will tend to follow where you want to go. They do this to remain close, maintaining those good feelings.

If you're smart, you pay attention to feelings. They are so powerful they quickly create or change attitudes and actions. They often have a lasting effect on what happens between people. Think about a time you met someone and came away with a "funny" feeling about him. You didn't know why. He spoke all the right words, but you still didn't like or trust him. You might even have felt a little sheepish, thinking you had no "good reason" for feeling the way you did. You may even have said, "I don't know why, but I just have this funny feeling about him." Chances are, later events verified your initial response.

EXERCISE

Think about those people with whom you most like to spend time. How do you feel when you're together?

Find the connection?

In one way or another, at one level or another, charismatic leaders have always understood this. *They don't depend on logic and rational argument to win over their followers.* They use techniques that appeal not to the brain but to the heart. Abraham Lincoln expressed the concept perfectly in 1842:

> If you would win a man to your cause, first convince him that you are his sincere friend [emphasis added]. Therein is a drop of honey that catches his heart, which, say what he will, is the great high road to his reason, and which, once gained, you will find but little trouble in convincing his judgement of the justice of your cause, if indeed that cause really be a just one .... Such is man, and so must he be understood by those who would lead him, even to his own best interest.

> *Charismatic leaders are responsible for making people feel comfortable, for caring enough to meet every person where they are. If you would have others follow you, first step toward them. Only then can you walk in the direction you choose, knowing they will follow.*

THE ONE LINK THAT BONDS PEOPLE TOGETHER

Virtually everything human beings do occurs in a rhythmic fashion. *All aspects of our behavior are synchronized with all elements of our activity.* The rhythms and intensity of our brain waves are like orchestra conductors for everything we do, think, and feel. Things like our thought processes, physical movements, healing ability, and speech patterns coincide with internally related rhythms.

Yet, outside the scientific community, few people ever consider what incredibly rhythmic creatures we are. Cultural anthropologist Edward T. Hall said in *The Dance of Life*, "I discovered a system of behavior going on under our very noses about which virtually nothing was known. Unfolding before my very eyes was a perpetual ballet."

Rhythm is fundamental to communication. When we speak, we do so with a certain rhythm. By extension, our breathing does the same. We gesture in response to our thoughts. Our words create synchrony with our expressions and gestures, our speech and movement are coordinated down to the finest detail.

These natural rhythms form the basis for all connection. *Before we can link with another, there must first be synchrony between us.* It is our bodies and voices moving in rhythmic harmony with others' that creates synchrony. This is the foundation upon which all positive relationships are built.

Rhythm itself is a form of communication. It carries our messages back and forth like the electrical impulses sent across telephone lines. *It is believed to be the channel humans use to communicate affinity and trust to one another.* This communication occurs so deep within us and is so extraordinarily subtle we are usually unaware of it. Yet, extensive scientific examination shows *it may be one of the most powerful forces connecting us as human beings.*

When one person's rhythm syncs with another's, a deep harmony exists between them. Their positive interaction generates mutual good feeling and comfort. Synchrony is the natural by-product. *If you are unable to attain this level of synchrony, you experience discord.* There is an abrasive quality to your dealings. Yet, you are unable to discern why.

This is because, as people converse, their bodies move together in a rhythmic motion. The result is a synchronous "dance," encompassing either a portion of or their entire bodies. At times one person controls the dance. At other times the lead shifts, drawing the two in new directions.

If you remember learning to dance, you recall being told, the man always leads. Once we actually begin to dance, however, something else becomes apparent. Although technically the man always leads, his partner can usually move them to where she wants to be on the dance floor. She doesn't push or pull or verbalize directions to him. Somehow they just end up there. This is the art of synchrony.

As a couple dance, they develop a rhythm and begin to move comfortably together (a form of entrainment). The woman's desire to shift direction can be subtly communicated through their rhythm. Because there is enjoyment in the smooth rhythm between them, the man will move in another direction if he senses she wants to do so.

Synchronizing with the natural rhythms of others builds an almost unbreakable connection between people. It allows you to create acceptance and trust. Once you learn to tap into this striking element of human behavior, leadership becomes a simple process.

Edward Hall was one of the first to discover this pervasive synchronous communication. In his book *Beyond Culture* he describes the work of his colleagues and himself:

> Movies by Condon and Birdwhistell as well as my own taken in a variety of settings and circumstances, reveal that when two people talk to each other their movements are synchronized. Sometimes this occurs in barely perceptible ways when finger, eyelid blinking and head movements occur simultaneously and in sync with specific parts of the verbal code (the words with pitches and stresses) as it unwinds. In other cases, the

whole body moves as though the two were under the control of a master choreographer who has written what Lawrence Halprin calls an open score.

The synchronous dance is unmistakable. As two friends sit and talk, there is a rhythmic quality to their voices. The tempo of their speech is the same. Many aspects of their physiology match. Their postures may be the same. Their gestures move in synchrony. Even the movements easiest to overlook (such as the rate of blinking, the tapping of a finger, and the rate of breath) are in perfect synchrony with the other. At some deep level this rhythmic communication weaves a tapestry interlacing others into the same pattern.

When our rhythmic behavior goes into sync with another's, the bond is deep. That's because our every thought, breath, and movement is in rhythmic synchrony with the sweeping patterns of our brain waves. *Being able to fall into sync with virtually anyone is the gift that allows charismatic leaders to so smoothly deal with almost any situation.* It is the foundation of that human quality we call grace.

Studying this phenomenon is difficult. Because our culture completely overlooks such experiences in our daily lives, synchrony is even difficult to explain. It's strange that our language should not have the vocabulary to adequately describe a phenomenon that is a controlling factor in our every interaction.

Further, the incredible number of ways in which we synchronize with one another is subtle. Special filming techniques and long analysis in a time/motion analyzer are needed to observe synchrony at all its levels. This kind of analysis has been done in a wide variety of cultures and situations.

What these studies show is that *human synchrony touches us at a basic level from the moment of birth.* The newborn infant moves in wonderful synchrony with his or her mother's voice. This phenomenon continues to permeate our lives.

Soon, several things became apparent. Conversation was continuous. It never stopped. Yet the content was not highly relevant. They were talking to be talking. If the conversation lagged, the work lagged. Two or three men could work in a very small area without ever seeming to interfere with each other, though they worked very close together. Whether adobe bricks were being laid, plaster was being applied to the walls or cement was being smoothed, the whole operation was like a ballet with the rhythm of the conversation providing the unconscious score that strengthened the group bond and kept them from interfering with each other [emphasis added]. (Hall, 1976)

EXERCISE

Begin to notice the powerful bonding effect rhythmic interactions have on people all around you.

- **The marching chant of a group of protestors.**
- **Children's rhymes that are used to control the repetitive rhythms of their games (such as jump rope).**
- **The rhythmic litanies of religious groups.**
- **The "Wave" at a sports stadium.**
- **The persuasive cadences of political speeches.**

We can catch a glimpse of rhythm's power by observing its effect on those no longer having full neurological functioning. In these people we see the almost magical transformations rhythm creates.

In *The Man Who Mistook His Wife For A Hat* Dr. Oliver Sacks reviews the case of a nineteen-year-old girl named Rebecca. Referred to Dr. Sacks by her grandmother, Rebecca was described as being extremely clumsy, a "motor moron."

She was a spastic who could spend hours trying to shove a foot into the wrong shoe. Rebecca would walk into walls or doors as if she didn't know they were there. Her movements were jerky, erratic, and uncouth. Sadly, she had a fine mind trapped in a body over which she had very little control. When talking with her, Dr. Sacks couldn't help but be touched by her fluid and graceful thinking. But her mind was somehow unable to reach and conduct the workings of her body.

Yet, when introduced to music, Rebecca danced as fluidly and gracefully as she thought, all hesitancy, all clumsiness gone. Her body flowed as elegantly as her mind. With the rhythmically dominated medium of music, her body and mind found a new way to communicate. By following the path of the music, she came to her full self.

This is a common phenomenon for thousands who have lost a portion of their neurological control. Everyday routines may be grinding chores. But they somehow find wholeness when bathed in waves of a dominant rhythm.

> Their uncouth movements may disappear in a moment with music and dancing—suddenly, with music, they know how to move. We see how the retarded, unable to perform fairly simple tasks involving perhaps four or five movements or procedures in sequence, can do these perfectly if they work to music—the sequence of movements they cannot hold as schemes being perfectly holdable as music, i.e., embedded in music. (Sacks, 1970)

If you pay attention, you'll notice that *small talk in business and social settings is far more important in maintaining synchrony than is avoiding uncomfortable silent periods*. In fact, silence among individuals who are already in sync seems to create no discomfort at all, regardless of setting.

> ***Human synchrony is a form of communication in and of itself. It is the language of human trust, affinity, and bonding.***

The small talk of a group at a cocktail party creates a rhythmic bond. *The content of what is said isn't nearly as important as the comfortable rhythmic pace.* The pace is what brings the group together. If members of the group fall silent, *it is the loss of group rhythm that creates the discomfort far more than the silence does.*

We've all known one of those uncomfortable moments when someone attempts to interject new conversation that dies and makes everyone even more uncomfortable. In such situations either the synchrony of the group has been destroyed or the attempted input did not match the rhythm of the group.

> It is striking how belatedly we have discovered the obvious. Any dancer or musician could have told us that we must share a common rhythm to sing or play or dance together. So could any athlete who plays on a team. And, privately we have always known that a common rhythmicity is essential to consummate sexual union. But why didn't we realize earlier that interaction rhythms were essential in every human interaction? Are scientists always the last to know what artists and others have known all along? (Scheflen, 1982)

Undoubtedly, *synchrony is a powerful influence on human behavior.* There is, however, a wide range to the levels of connection that can be created. Sometimes small amounts of synchrony between people develops only marginal comfort between them. At other times, a truly profound bond can be created. *The bond can so deeply attach one to another that much of one person's internal physiology is actually being directed by someone else.*

> **Good conversationalists aren't only adept at introducing topics but also at maintaining the rhythm of the conversation.**

While synchrony is occurring outside us, something is happening within. *Once we are in sync for awhile, the neurolog-*

ical connection we call entrainment is established. It was William Condon who devised a number of experiments that resulted in the remarkable discovery that *the nervous system of one person can literally drive that of another.*

> In one striking experiment, two people in conversation were wired to EEG's to see if there was any comparability in brain waves. Two cameras were set up so that one focused on the speakers, the other on the EEG recording pens. When the two people talked the recording pens moved together as though driven by a single brain. When one of the individuals was pulled out of the conversation by a third person, the pens no longer moved together. Fantastic, isn't it? Yet the data are incontrovertible. (Hall, 1976)

What this and additional experiments by other researchers uncovered was that when two or more people move into a deep level of synchrony, far more than their external bodies function in harmony. Their nervous systems do too. Our brain and nervous system infuse emotions, allow us to think, and store our memories. They are the essence of us. They can be, and often do, become connected in some still unknown way with others. This profound relationship is entrainment, the phenomenon utilized by great charismatic leaders.

> *Deep human synchrony is the outward manifestation of entrainment, the neurological connection between humans.*

EXERCISE

Next time you're with a group of friends notice the rhythm of the conversation. Everyone will be talking at the same rate of speed.

ENTRAINMENT: THE ESSENCE OF A
MAGNETIC PERSONALITY

Although connecting with others is a basic part of being human, most people do it on a hit-or-miss basis. They never *purposefully* use the 93 percent of communication occurring outside conscious awareness. Sadly, they never come even close to realizing the full power of their natural abilities.

However, *using entrainment, you can learn to transmit natural leadership through all levels of the communication process.* You can then communicate sameness at such a deep level you won't need to mimic others or use contrived leadership processes. A rhythmic interaction between yourself and the other person becomes the basis for a more straightforward and comfortable communication.

Remember our innate need to feel comfortable with others, and our natural tendency to feel comfortable around people who are like us. When people are like us, we feel safe, trusting, and open. These good feelings cause us to like those people and want to be around them. This is the process you want the people with whom you communicate to go through with you. In other words, you want to create entrainment. This profound connection weaves a deep fabric of trust, harmony, and affinity. People then follow your leadership as comfortably as they snuggle beneath a soft, warm blanket on a cold winter night.

Entrainment is a term coined by researcher William Condon. It traditionally has been used to describe a phenomenon that occurs in both the physical and organic worlds. It describes how *similar moving objects, animate and inanimate, tend to move in rhythmic synchrony.* Fireflies moving close to one another blink in unison. Put two grandfather clocks with the same size pendulum next to one another. They will eventually move in synchrony—regardless of the rhythm with which they started. Even electronic oscillators will entrain to the fastest frequency if their initial frequencies are close enough.

Entrainment occurs naturally in humans when one person's movements, actions, and words fall into a rhythmic synchrony with another. We can tell people have entrained when their physical behavior (gestures, tempo of speech, and so forth) are in sync with one another. The problem with natural entrainment is that there are times when no matter how hard we try, we can't "connect" with another person. By using syncing skills—which parallel what occurs when people are naturally in sync—we allow the natural phenomenon to kick in.

What happens when people entrain? Well, for starters, both people feel close to each other at a deep and fundamental level. There is a strong inclination to implicitly trust each other, even if they have only just met. In addition, when one changes the subject, interjects new thoughts, or changes his or her emotional state of mind, the other person moves right along.

For example, say Mary and Paul are entrained and talking about the past week's business activity. Suddenly, Mary remembers she is going to pick up her new car the next day and had forgotten to tell Paul. As Mary excitedly talks about the car, Paul will automatically become excited himself.

Is Paul excited because of Mary's impending purchase? Maybe or maybe not. In normal situations, he could just as well be envious, disinterested, or even judgmental about the purchase. Yet, if the two are entrained it really doesn't matter. When Mary makes an emotional shift, Paul follows automatically, without thinking about it. They are close enough at that moment to keep negative thoughts out of the picture.

Here's how it happens. *Each of us has brain waves constantly pulsating in a rhythmic fashion. Different frequencies produce different responses and behaviors in us.* It's as though a pebble dropped in the ponds of our minds sends ripples throughout our entire body. There are certain rhythmic patterns of brain waves that allow us to sleep and even to enter different stages of sleep. There are the rhythmic patterns that help create different emotional states. For example, when human beings are depressed they tend to have a fairly slow progression of brain waves. But when we become excited, our brain waves pulsate in rapid succession.

These varied rhythmic patterns act very much as an orchestra conductor for our entire mental, physical, and emotional responses. For this reason, entrainment—the ability to drive the frequency of others' neuroprocessing—can allow a leader to have a profound impact on those he or she leads.

Although we still don't know why entrainment occurs or what actual vehicle creates the connection, *we can create it at will.* This isn't as frightening as it may sound. In fact, it's been happening to you since you were born. More important, you have been entraining with others your whole life.

Think about a time when someone close to you yawned and you uncontrollably followed suit. Yet, on other occasions when someone near you yawned it had no impact on you at all. What was the difference? Simple. In the first case you had naturally entrained with the other person. Her yawn automatically spawned the same behavior in you because that deep connection had already taken place. In the second case, you hadn't entrained so nothing pulled you to follow her movement.

Yawning is considered by some researchers to be purely psychological. Triggered by a "yawn detector" in the brain, yawning is believed by some to be an evolutionary adaptation. In our primitive days, it helped us to synchronize our wake/sleep pattern to *keep our social group on the same wave length.*

Everyone successfully entrains with others at different times. But because entrainment is created and maintained at a deep level, most people have little or no control over their success rate. Left to its own natural course, entrainment is unpredictable. It may occur instantly, or within three to five minutes, or possibly never.

When entrainment occurs it is often expressed in statements like:

Five minutes after I met her I felt I had known her all my life. I knew she was exactly right for this project.

I'd only met him once before in that big negotiating session, but I had no problem giving him all the information he asked for. I knew he'd do right by us.

I had had a lot of misgivings about the money being spent on that new training, but after talking with the consultant I realized he's just what we've needed to get everyone on track and pulling together. He's dynamite!

I just met with the new CEO. You know, I wonder why I had ever worried about her. She's the best thing that ever happened to this company. I can't wait to get going on the projects we talked about.

Our ability to make friends, put others at ease, and be successful at getting our points across is predicated on this unpredictable phenomenon. However, *entrainment is too important for leaders to leave to chance.* You must be able to consistently coalesce individuals and groups to your leadership. You need to do it quickly and at will. *You must know how to rhythmically, emotionally, and physically become like the other person—no matter who the other person is.*

Entrainment involves more than finding common ground by saying the right words or talking about the right subjects. While most people are casting their conversational lines into the water hoping for a nibble, truly charismatic leaders are gathering up others in a net woven of far more powerful methods.

> *Entrainment is like hitching a trailer to a car. Once the connection is made the trailer will follow in any direction.*

And you guessed it, throughout history charismatic leaders have been entraining thousand upon thousands of their followers without even knowing what it was they were doing. In fact, *entrainment is probably the very essence of the "magnetic personality" these individuals seem to possess.*

The more people are entrained the more they will listen to the other's ideas and follow his or her direction. They tend to embrace that person's leadership in a natural and enthusiastic manner. *People will continue to follow that leadership naturally and happily as long as it's proper and ethical.*

With this kind of power, it seems that charismatic leaders could manipulate followers to do virtually anything they desired. On first glance, this appears true. There are, however, two things that pull people instantly out of entrainment. *No matter how deeply you have entrained with another, if you become incongruent or violate one of his or her beliefs or values, the connection is instantly snapped.*

Entrainment is sustained only as long as you're communicating honesty and not attempting to go against the others' beliefs and values. In this way, entrainment is a powerful tool for all forms of leadership. But it can be successfully used only when the direction in which the leader is moving is in the best interest of those involved. By mastering the simple syncing skills in the following two chapters you, too, can possess this most powerful of leadership capabilities.

In Short

1. Charismatic leadership depends first on your ability to get others to accept you and your position.
2. Charismatic leaders create a profound closeness or connection with those they lead. Known by some as the "likability factor," this is often the result of a rhythmic interaction set up by the leader.
3. Rhythm is a powerful form of human communication in and of itself.
4. Human synchrony is the outward manifestation of the more profound human connection called entrainment. When people entrain, there is a still-to-be defined level of neurological connection that creates a powerful bond between people. This bond is so deep others will hap-

pily follow your leadership in order not to sever the connection.

5. Though entrainment is a naturally occurring phenomenon, it can be created and maintained at will. This, of course, is predicated on the fact that you are congruent (honest in your intent) and don't violate the others' beliefs or values.

5

THE TEN TECHNIQUES
OF LIKABILITY

One pervasive misnomer is the saying that "information is power." In fact, information is rather useless unless one knows precisely what to do with it. The phenomenon of entrainment is no exception. As powerful as it is, the mere understanding of its effect is of little use without the precise knowledge of how to implement it into your life. Chapters 4, 5, and 6 are dedicated to giving you the true power of entrainment: the ability to bring it to life.

BRINGING THE SECRET TO LIFE

The fastest way to entrain someone is to move into rhythmic synchrony with him or her. We as human beings are constantly moving, breathing, and speaking in accordance with different internal or external rhythms. *To sync with someone you simply have to match any one or a series of the rhythms that person is living by at that time.*

Within the full spectrum of human communication there are a variety of behaviors that can be synced with in order to entrain people. Syncing creates a rhythmic sameness between people, establishing levels of compatibility within minutes. Most important, *syncing communicates sameness to both the conscious and the unconscious minds of anyone at any time.*

The list below comprises only a few of the behaviors you can utilize.

Some behaviors you can sync with are

    Speaking rate

    Breathing

    Walking

    Various physical rhythms

Watch two friends engrossed in conversation. Notice their postures. They usually will be identical. The people may be unaware of it, but *their connection is expressed in every aspect of their physiology.* Their gestures, vocal quality, and facial expressions will usually be the same or similar because they are communicating at both the conscious and the unconscious level. They have entrained.

We can *consciously* follow the path laid down by this natural process to vastly expand our leadership abilities. Let's say a person is sitting across from us at a meeting. To create entrainment, you may begin speaking at the same tempo. By extension, this begins to sync your breathing rates.

By adhering to this simple concept, within minutes your bodies will begin to naturally move into physical synchrony. You will notice that your sitting positions become similar. Your facial expressions and gestures will become more alive and expansive. The overall intensity of the conversation will increase. Entrainment shortly follows. Continue to verbally communicate. You have laid the foundation for a far more profound level of communication to take place naturally. All you must do is start the process and nature will take it from there.

TWO-STEP TEST FOR ENTRAINMENT: KNOWING WHEN TO ASSERT YOUR LEADERSHIP

Entrainment enables you to lead people more effectively. It can develop total acceptance from others. They gladly listen to what you say and feel comfortable following your leadership. It's probably the best way to reduce others' prejudices and barriers and get them to openly consider and accept your ideas and direction.

Leaders are always trying to move people in new directions, interject new ideas, and make suggestions. The process of syncing can make this part of your job remarkably simple. Once you gain entrainment with others, they want to preserve the unconscious bond. They like the feeling entrainment creates.

It is critical for you to know precisely when you have reached entrainment with another person. It is only then that you are able to comfortably lead them. Fortunately, there are physical traits that correspond with the level of connection you have developed with another. Using this two-step process as a test, you will know if it's time to assert your leadership or to continue matching or syncing.

Step #1

How do we as human beings know if we like, trust, or respect someone? What is it that lets us know? Quite simply, it is a certain feeling we have toward someone we have classified at the unconscious level as likable or worthy of trust or respect.

As we know, feelings are a way our unconscious relays information to our conscious mind after it has processed a huge amount of information about a person. This is a sophisticated form of communication between the conscious and unconscious minds. We recall being around people we didn't like and others to whom we felt attracted—both for no apparent reason. This can be confusing if you don't know the reason for these seemingly random feelings.

In order to know that your syncing efforts are working, you must be aware of your own feelings during the process. When you sync with someone, the feeling you have should be the same as when you're around a friendly acquaintance. This feeling should start within the first thirty seconds after beginning to sync. When you get this feeling, you can be sure the other person is experiencing it too. You are on your way to developing entrainment.

Step #2

The most critical indicator that entrainment has been created is when the person you've been syncing with begins physically to follow your movements. Whether you have spoken or not, the person will follow when you change some part of your behavior. For example, if you have been syncing her breathing rate and begin to slow yours down, hers should also slow. If the two of you have been speaking at the same rate of speed for some minutes, then you sit up in your chair and they do the same you know you're entrained.

When the two unconscious minds are sufficiently entrained the other person unconsciously adjusts her body and rhythmic behavior to remain similar to yours. The other person will begin to follow you both at the verbal and non-verbal level in order to maintain the comfortable feeling of entrainment. Test this last indicator. Once you have reached this step you have created entrainment. It is then time to assert your leadership and comfortably lead the other person.

Should you fail to achieve any one of the indicators simply go back and sync an additional behavior or two for a few minutes. Then go through the testing process again. With a little practice, you will find you seldom have to sync someone more than once to develop entrainment.

FOUR WAYS TO MAKE THE PROFOUND CONNECTION

Syncing skills provide the direct path to entrainment. Naturally mastered by virtually every great charismatic leader, they quickly create profound connection with virtually anyone in minutes. All these skills are interchangeable and can be used one at a time or in conjunction with several. In addition, any rhythmic behavior can be used to sync with any other rhythmic behavior. Once you understand them feel free to play with them.

Speaking Rate

The tempo or rhythm of your speech is one of your most important entraining tools. As you will see in the next chapter, voice tempo and rhythm can have a stunning impact upon thousands of people at a time. Yet, in one-on-one interaction, syncing your tempo or rate of speech with another person's can be a wonderful bridge for moving you down the path of entrainment. Have you ever talked to someone who spoke much faster or slower than you? It was uncomfortable, because there was no synchrony, no entrainment.

Rhythm is a means by which the listener can be drawn into the words of the speaker, participating in the immediate contact and thus joining the subjective experience and point of view of the speaker. A "moving" argument may be exactly that. By linking the synchrony of body and ideas, parallel physiologic changes begin to occur. The original rhythm of all music is the heartbeat (before the invention of the metronome, musicians used the resting heartbeat as a baseline). Conversational synchrony, absorbing narrative, and a gradual unfolding of emotional experiences are reflected in physiologic, emotional, and cognitive changes. (Brown, 1991)

To sync with someone using this technique, simply talk at approximately the same tempo as the other person. If he normally uses a slow, dragging tempo, slow yours down as well. Should he have one of those faster-than-a-speeding-bullet tempos, synchronize to it. Remember, even if it is uncomfortable for you in the first few minutes, once entrainment occurs you can gradually alter the rate to one more comfortable for you. The other person will then naturally follow.

EXERCISE

Make a point of taking one day to consciously speak at roughly the same rate of speed as everyone you come into contact with. You'll be amazed at how much people warm up to you and how quickly your proficiency will grow.

Also, note when you are in a location with music playing in the background. Invariably people have synced to it. When addressing a small group or making a presentation, it's a good idea to begin in sync with this background music. In this way, you are likely in sync with a rhythm already established within everyone in the room.

Breathing

Breathing is one of the most controlling elements of our physiology. It generates a penetrating rhythm throughout our bodies. From it, all other physical movement reacts. The unconscious mind is acutely aware of breathing rate and the level of synchrony between it and others. Therefore, it is the most potent element of physiology with which we can sync.

This most powerful tool for developing entrainment is not obtrusive and seems to be one of the most powerful behaviors to sync from a distance. This may seem to be an unusual aspect of human behavior to concentrate on while speaking with someone. Yet, it is a fairly common part of other cultures.

> One clue is that the Japanese are more aware of synchrony than the average Westerner. Those tremendous Sumo wrestlers, for example, must synchronize their breathing before the referee will allow the match to begin, and the audience is fully aware of what is happening. In this same vein, Japanese who are conversing will frequently monitor their own breathing in order to stay in sync with their interlocutor. (Hall, 1983)

This technique is powerful. *In fact, there are negotiators who bring associates to negotiations with them whose sole function is to sync the breathing rates of those on the other side of the table.*

EXERCISE

If you want to be convinced as to the natural power of this phenomenon and at the same time develop your own proficiency, try this exercise.

Get a partner and stand face-to-face, 6 to 8 inches apart. Stare into each other's eyes for 3 to 5 minutes. Within seconds, your peripheral vision will begin to detect your partner's breathing rate through the rise and fall of his or her shoulders. Within the first 90 seconds, you will notice your breathing rates fall naturally into synchrony. When you feel entrainment has developed, break it by changing your breathing rate. It will feel uncomfortable. You will experience a strong natural pull to reestablish the entrainment.

After a seminar in Washington, D.C, we were approached by a young counterintelligence agent who already had a reputation of note. He was dissatisfied because his superior never accepted the initiatives he presented. He felt his ideas weren't given serious consideration due to his youthfulness.

He was happy to describe what occurred during interactions between him and his boss, especially those in which he was turned down. Normally, he sat in front of his boss's desk, explaining his idea fully. When he finished, his boss would lean back in his chair, put his hands behind his head and think it over. After four or five minutes, his boss would invariably come up with a reason to reject the idea. It didn't matter how thorough and convincing the young agent thought he had been.

We gave the agent a crash course in matching posture, gestures, and breathing rate and showed him the indicators of entrainment. He later told us what happened the next time he proposed an initiative. He presented everything in the same manner as before. When his boss leaned back in the chair, however, the agent did not nervously wait for an answer. He simply synced with his boss.

He too sat back casually in his chair and placed his hands behind his head. Using peripheral vision, he noted his boss's breathing rate and adjusted his to match. After thinking for a few minutes, the boss sat forward and said, "Okay, kid, I'll give you a shot." The agent continues to use syncing skills and every viable initiative he brings forward has been accepted.

If you have difficulty detecting the breathing rhythms of others, there are several simple things you can do. First, remember that people exhale while speaking. You can detect their breathing pattern just by listening to them talk. Also, try looking at a stationary spot behind and just above the person's shoulder. As you gaze at that point, your peripheral vision will detect the rise and fall of the shoulder. This gives you the person's breathing rate.

Walking

If there are human beings present, you can be assured there are a variety of rhythms present. Never overlook the dominant rhythms in any endeavor. Consider walking. Often people grab every available second by working while on the move. Not only can talking something over while walking together save time, it can actually facilitate coming to agreement.

"Let's take a walk around the block and talk it over," we might say at a sticky point in a dealing with a co-worker. If you entrain with the other's walking rhythm, chances are you will be able to get past the sticking point.

In the movie *Dead Poets Society* the character played by Robin Williams asks a group of his students to walk around the perimeter of a school courtyard. He doesn't tell them why he wants them to do this. As the group begins walking, each has his own individual stride, gait, or walking rhythm. Yet within moments, the group of boys are walking in perfect synchrony and continue the walk in this fashion. The teacher played by Williams said he wanted to show the innate desire for conformity. What it actually demonstrated was a perfect example of natural entrainment. *When two or more people are together doing similar things, they will entrain.*

EXERCISE

Next time you're at a bypass with someone or tempers are beginning to flare stop everything! Get out of the office and take a walk with the other person. You'll find that the discussion goes far better. Not only do you get some fresh air and have the opportunity to stretch, but the act of walking will begin to throw both of you into sync.

Remember, every behavior a human performs— whether it's talking, walking, eating, sleeping, or breathing—has an inherent rhythm directing it. If you quickly sync with the most profound rhythmic behavior, you will create entrainment between the two of you. You don't even have to do it at the same time the other does it; just maintain the same general rhythm.

Various Rhythms

Have you ever seen someone who is almost continuously tapping a foot or finger while talking to you? That's as clear a rhythm as anyone will ever give you. These particular types of rhythms have to do with something going on inside the other person.

Suppose you are meeting with a potential client and he continuously taps a foot. These kinds of rhythms don't necessarily have any conscious meaning to the person exhibiting them. If others think about it at all, they often believe it indicates nervousness. In fact, the tapping foot may be a way the person synchronizes his own personal rhythms, enjoys music, or releases excess energy.

Syncing with these obvious rhythms can be beneficial to the entrainment process. If someone is tapping his foot, you might tap your foot, finger, or pencil in sync. You can even talk in sync with that rhythm for awhile. It really doesn't matter what you use as long as you match the rhythm. Anytime you mimic you can get in trouble, so be careful of being too obvious.

EXERCISE

Think of human interactions as a symphony of intertwining rhythms. As in any orchestra, regardless of the instrument you're playing, it's imperative that you do so in rhythm with the rest of the instruments. Next time you're chatting with someone try syncing with a variety of the other person's rhythmic behaviors. Feel free to play!

In the same way some people tap their finger, others lightly sway their body while standing. This rhythm is also one that can be synced in a variety of ways. In small groups at social gatherings you can often find everyone in the group slightly swaying side to side. That is the group's rhythm. All conversation syncs to it.

Syncing and Leading Overview

1. Select a rhythmic behavior(s) to match or sync in the other person.

2. After three to five minutes, test the degree of entrainment by leading nonverbally.

3. Adjust your body or ask the other person to do something simple you want him or her to do.

4. If you meet resistance, start the process all over to entrain more deeply.

5. Sync additional behaviors.

6. Retest by leading and ask again in another way.

Developing the sensitivity necessary to create strong entrainment requires a few weeks of concerted training. Becoming more sensitive to others' rhythmic behavior enables you to quickly affect them at the unconscious level. To speed your learning process, practice any of these skills in a relaxed manner each day.

SIX MORE WAYS TO QUICKLY GENERATE LIKABILITY

Another set of related skills have received a good deal of attention over the past decade. Called matching, these have been extolled as the road to highly successful human interactions. However, such skills are only the beginning, another dash of spice in the main dish of entrainment.

Powerful leaders entrain those who follow them. Matching someone's physiology or ideas can lead to a comfortable interaction that helps establish synchrony. They do not of themselves create entrainment. The reason is that matching and mirroring tends to be somewhat static in their applications. However, synchrony follows the flowing and ever-changing interaction of humans.

Matching can be used in much the same way as you use your car key to start your car's engine. The turning of the key itself does not turn over the engine. What it does do is send the electrical current to the starter, which activates the engine. Matching someone tends to move you toward natural synchronous movement and thus to entrainment. However, it can be the long way around.

You can match more than rhythms to help synchronize with others. Matching behaviors may be helpful as you begin to build synchrony. If the other person crosses his right leg, you cross yours. If he rests his right elbow on the table, you rest your right elbow also. If he leans forward, so do you.

Matching can be effective because it mimics natural human behavior. Remember, though, it is not subtle. When matching occurs naturally, it happens outside of conscious awareness of both participants. The movements are effective because they are subtle. When consciously choosing these actions, you risk drawing attention to them with your conversation becoming awkward and uncomfortable.

The following lists reveal many of the ways people unconsciously communicate "sameness" to one another. You may use any to match or sync in any combination to begin the entrainment process in virtually any situation.

Some behaviors that can be matched

    Posture

    Gestures

    Vocal qualities

    Beliefs and values

    Key words and phrases

    Mood

Posture

One of the simplest behaviors to match is posture. It can easily be matched alone, in conjunction with other behaviors, or when you have no verbal interaction.

People who have naturally developed entrainment tend to lean at the same angles: either to the side, forward, or back. If someone is hunched over, for example, lean forward. If she is standing straight and erect, do the same. The things to look for when matching someone's postural characteristics are

Leaning -	forward
	back
	or to the side
Head tilt -	forward
	back
	or to the side
Shoulders -	Are they back?
	Slumped?
	Pushed up?

EXERCISE

To quickly develop your intuitive ability for matching posture and broad physical behaviors get a partner and try the following exercise.

Have the partner stand a certain way and hold that posture while you match it as thoroughly as possible. Then close your eyes and have the partner adjust his or her stance. Open your eyes and determine how the partner changed position by once again matching the partner's posture.

Begin with broad changes, then gradually become more and more subtle as your skill develops.

Matching any or all of these characteristics can greatly assist in entrainment. When working with posture, however, always subtlely move toward matching the other person. Abrupt shifts are likely to be consciously detected and noted.

Gestures

Similar hand, facial, or body gestures used to emphasize similar points can effectively communicate sameness. We all know people who make expressive use of their body when speaking. Their gestures have a tremendous amount of deep meaning to them. When you speak, use gestures similar to the ones they used when talking. *Be careful not to mimic.* Some people gesture in front of their bodies while others may make wide arcs to their sides. Though you don't want to gesture at the same time they do or in exactly the same way, it is usually fine to simply gesture generally the same way they do.

Most of us have been told at one time or another to sit up straight and look attentive when talking with others. This advice is well meaning but inappropriate. For example, a variety of studies over the last twenty years have shown that *people are hired far more on the basis of personality than on qualifications. In fact, the person who is better liked is often hired over much more qualified people.* In the interview process, it is far more important that the interviewer perceives you as compatible rather than as someone with good posture.

The same holds true in all our dealings. Generating likability is important to success. Consider the use of matching to help speed up the entrainment process. Your chances of making the sale, getting the donation or job, or winning over a voter are greatly enhanced.

Match posture, facial expressions, gestures, or even the tilt of the head. Within moments, you will see and feel the indicators of entrainment taking place. Once you can lead physically, you can comfortably assert yourself in the situation. This is the time to explain your position or make your proposal.

Vocal Quality

Matching someone's tone and volume of voice is also helpful in establishing entrainment. Surprisingly, most Americans don't discern subtle changes in vocal quality. Few have developed an ear sensitive enough to detect such changes. This is probably because so many people are now highly dependent on visual processing.

For many Americans television is the leading medium of influence and the primary vehicle of social communication. Television bypasses the subtleties of human interaction, using powerful images and music to stimulate emotion. We have become conditioned to bright, flashy pictures, loud, driving music and obvious language aimed at inducing strong fluctuations in our emotions. Through mass-media presentations, Americans have been conditioned to overlook many of the subtleties of life. The unconscious mind, however, is still acutely aware of these subtleties and continues to act on them.

Tone of voice can be high and squeaky or low and gravelly. It can be melodic and sing-song or flat and dull. As long as someone's tone isn't too distinctive and unique, adjusting your tone to match can be powerful. This particular skill takes a little work, but the results are well worth it.

Volume of voices also ranges considerably. Let's suppose a man with a booming voice and another who is soft-spoken are trying to settle an issue in the office. Although each is being polite, they appear to be having difficulty finding common ground. The most noticeable difference between the two is the volume of their voices.

Suppose one man speaks to the other in a voice loud enough to be heard throughout the department. The other speaks almost in a whisper. Both would soon become frustrated. One man would continue to quietly state his points. The other would boom out with "What?" "What did you say?" These two people don't know that when conversing with others (especially those with uniquely loud or soft voices) it's best to raise or lower our voice to match. It's an easy way to make others feel more comfortable and help establish entrainment.

Beliefs and Values

Matching beliefs and values is important in entraining individuals and groups. Beliefs and values create our core programming, our way of looking at the world. Because they are so central to our lives we feel positive toward people who share or support them. The opposite is also true. When people confront or challenge our beliefs, we have a natural and strong negative reaction.

You can create entrainment by matching or validating beliefs and values without actually sharing them. Merely stating or repeating them back to a person creates a strong bond. We are able to gain a valuable connection without compromising our integrity.

People often verbalize their beliefs and values during even the most casual conversations. You just need to know what to listen for. Beliefs and values are usually expressed in strong statements such as "People are . . . ," "Life is . . . ," "I will always . . ."

The statements following these words contain a strong emotional impact for that person. By matching or validating their beliefs and values you can quickly move down the road to entrainment. With practice, it becomes relatively simple to match values and beliefs without necessarily agreeing with them. In the following examples a department head is confronted with disgruntled employees at a staff meeting.

EXAMPLE #1

EMPLOYEE: I can't see the company wasting money on these employee assistance programs. People should handle their own problems. Everyone should be able to take care of themselves.

MANAGER: It's true that companies today spend a great deal more money on employee support services than ever before. And to be frank, I sure don't see an end to it.

EXAMPLE #2

EMPLOYEE: People always find a way to do what they really want to do. The board could have figured a way to give us that raise if they really cared about the workers on the line.

MANAGER: Because the people on the line care so much about the company, they expect the board to care a lot about them. They would like to know why certain decisions are made—especially when those decisions affect the amount of money we earn. It's frustrating when we aren't personally told why decisions are made.

EXAMPLE #3

EMPLOYEE: I know you want me to put in a lot of overtime on this project, but I have a family. I will always be a human being first and an employee second. No job will ever come before my family.

MANAGER: You know, I've thought about those same issues myself. Sometimes I struggle with meeting my obligations to both my family and the company. Why don't we sit down together and see if we come up with ways to get this project done without affecting our family lives too much.

This skill is vital for charismatic leaders in all areas. It's especially needed for those who lead in emotionally laden areas. For example, people who volunteer often have a strong belief or value motivating them to donate time or services. If

you want to lead volunteers to their greatest efforts and keep
them motivated, you should listen carefully to what they say.
When you speak to them, you can then reflect back their
established beliefs and values, reminding them of their reasons for being involved.

An interaction might go like this:

VOLUNTEER: I just hate to see all this open land used
for housing without leaving any open
space. *People have to be in touch with nature
to be fully alive.* I sure wouldn't want my
kids growing up in a concrete jungle.
The problem is, *if you're going to get something done you have to do it yourself.*

COORDINATOR: (At a later time) I'm worried about the
kinds of conditions people are going to
be living in on the south side if we don't
get enough signatures on this ballot initiative. Those housing plans *don't allow
for a single living thing in nature. It won't
be like really living for those people, especially the kids. Unfortunately, if we don't do
anything about it, I doubt anyone else will.*
Are you willing to get half of the signatures?

Notice that the coordinator does not repeat the exact
words of the volunteer. But by matching the expressed beliefs and values closely, the coordinator has established a
strong connection and refueled the volunteer's motivation.

Key Words and Phrases

Words are expressions of complex sets of thought, experiences, and feelings. Social groups, as well as the individuals in those groups, use certain words to describe unique
aspects of their lives and their experience of the world. These

---

EXERCISE

Some of the most powerful leaders we've dealt with, those who successfully deal with diverse interest groups, actually maintain notebooks detailing the beliefs and values of every group they interact with. In other words, they have at hand a listing of the most important issues for each of the groups they must influence.

Listen for strong statements from those you must influence from time to time. Keep a written log of those statements. Not only will it help you craft wonderfully powerful messages to them, but it will be like a map of a mine field keeping you from stepping in the wrong places.

---

words often become identified with specific groups of people, certain experiences. If you use the same words, you are connecting to many of their deep thoughts. A bond is created.

During different stages of our lives, we move from one social group to another. We then use different words to describe our current experience. Words that fit in at one stage or with one group simply don't work in another area. Remember words such as "groovy," "right on," "get down," and "I hear ya"? They once were common but now are dated, closely tied to a certain time and social group.

When we use the words and phrases of a person's current experience, we develop a stronger level of connection. Suppose someone often uses words such as "sensitive to," "in touch with," and "I feel like." If you use the same words or phrases back in another context, you help strengthen the link between you.

The conversation may go like this:

CUSTOMER: Look, I've been going over the *numbers* you gave me. I need to know they'll *hold* before I place the order. I have to keep my project *on target no matter what*. I need to be *assured* of your company's ability to *deliver product* at these estimates. Can you *hold* these *numbers* long enough to see our project through?

SALESPERSON: As a matter of fact, I just came from a staff meeting where we reviewed those *numbers*. Everyone is aware of your concerns. I've been *assured* of our ability to *hold*. There's no doubt we can *deliver product* that keeps you right *on target* throughout your project *no matter what*.

Also, every profession has its own vocabulary of buzz words and abbreviations. Such words are loaded with meaning and carry a rich set of associations. By appropriately using these words we again create a bond. Listen for these perfect matching tools.

Used appropriately, they fire off a complex set of thoughts or representations in the other person's mind. It creates a feeling of understanding between you and your listener. Very often the context in which professional jargon is used makes its meaning obvious. If it doesn't, ask the person using the word about its precise meaning. This enables you to properly use the word yourself and shows interest in the other's work.

Mood

If you are feeling depressed it can be difficult to entrain with someone who is overjoyed with life and vice versa. As a charismatic leader, it is your responsibility to sync with others. This means doing whatever it takes to entrain with them. You have to meet them where they are.

Mood, which is just another word for emotional state, manifests itself physiologically in a number of ways. It includes everything reviewed in this chapter. Think for a moment about people you've known who were defeated, completely down. Picture them. They were probably hunched over, their faces loose to the point of droopy, their breathing shallow. When they spoke it wasn't in a bright, fast-paced voice, but in a low, slow one.

Suppose you walk in to meet with Tom. You're there to discuss an upcoming project you'll be working on together. You don't know each other very well. Now, suppose when you walk into Tom's office you notice his face looks strained. He's frowning. He sighs as he stands up to greet you. His shoulders are slumped, and his smile is wane. When you shake hands, his grip is limp. His voice is flat.

If you move briskly about, smile broadly, and talk rapidly, what will happen? If you tell Tom what a beautiful day it is and how excited you are about this project, it's doubtful you'll develop entrainment. To connect with Tom, you must first become like him. Slow down. You should talk in a lower, flatter voice. Bend over slightly to match his posture.

Once you have entrained, you can slowly lead him out of his state and into one more conducive for your meeting. The leading process is quite simple. As entrainment is made with Tom, start gradually speaking more rapidly, begin moving in a more animated fashion. As you become more interested and enthusiastic about your topic, he will too. In essence, your presence, your ever-increasing mood will lead Tom out of his negative one.

Matching mood is really matching a number of behaviors. By developing your matching and syncing skills one at a time, you will soon be able naturally to assume the physiological traits of others without thinking about it. Great interpersonal communicators all have this skill. It brings them closer to people and increases comfort levels.

In Short

1. Entrainment can be created with another person by following the progression it naturally takes. This includes syncing and matching the natural rhythmic behavior communicated by another. Once a sufficient level of rhythmic behavior is created, entrainment develops.

2. There are a variety of behaviors that can be synced or matched. They include:

Category and Impact	Behavior
55% Physiology	Breathing
	Facial Expression
	Posture
	Gestures
	Rhythms
	Mood
38% Vocal Quality	Tempo
	Tone
	Volume
	Timbre
7% Words	Beliefs
	Values
	Key Words

3. There is a two-step process for determining if entrainment has occurred. Once you have been syncing or matching another for three to five minutes note if you have a comfortable feeling toward him or her and toward the interaction. If so, move on to the second step by making a subtle shift of your body. If the other person follows your movements, then entrainment has occurred. If you haven't successfully reached either of the steps, begin syncing or matching additional behaviors.

6

HOW TO CAPTURE THE HEARTS OF MILLIONS

People want to "experience" their leaders, like and believe in them. They want to follow a direction that "feels" right because the person providing the direction "feels" right. People are drawn to charismatic leaders for these reasons, not because they provide information or monitor direction.

Being liked and accepted isn't a nice perk we provide others, nor is it an advantage we unfairly give ourselves. *Likability is essential.* With it we develop a harmonious environment where people feel close and comfortable. This gives them a joyous eagerness to do their best. We are able to affect others emotionally, moving them to action. In other words, we are leaders in the most elegant sense of the word.

All leaders are managers. But not all managers are leaders. Management is a function comprised of regulations and administration. It requires only that you maintain control over a process. You are given authority along with the job title. *Respect and the ability to inspire are won only through your own efforts.* Being a true leader means more than managing people and resources. Remember the natural yearning of humans for closeness and the search for passion in their lives. *When you are able to give people what they most desire, they more willingly accept your ideas and leadership.*

In Chapter 5, we looked at techniques for developing deep levels of acceptance and likability with individuals. At times it's necessary to gracefully bring larger groups under our leadership. In this chapter, we consider techniques of entrainment that work quickly with groups of twenty or more. Other, even more powerful techniques, are effective with groups of 100, 100,000, and up.

Once mastered, these techniques firmly establish your leadership position. They require only a few minutes to coalesce a group, work team, company, or in many cases, entire countries. When you need to reestablish or generate greater acceptance, you simply reemploy any one or a combination of the techniques. Although each of these techniques are defined separately for clarification purposes, there is no ranking as to level of effectiveness. Use those with which you are most comfortable. Feel free to combine them in any way. They can even be effectively employed simultaneously. Remember, these techniques are all effective and share the same goal. If you are comfortable establishing acceptance and likability with individuals, you are ready to entrain with groups of people.

LEADERSHIP IN THE BOARDROOM: THE TWO-MINUTE TECHNIQUE

Whether your career is management, selling, fund raising, training, or politics, your ability to influence and lead groups is critical to your success. For example, many careers are made and broken in the conference room. There, discussion, negotiating, or brainstorming almost always results in interplays for leadership and the acceptance of ideas. Some people have a constant struggle just to stay in the race. However, there are always those who move ahead of the pack. They negotiate virtually unscathed on a track others find twisting and treacherous. In truth, *moving to the top without confrontation can be surprisingly simple.*

Next time you are before or among a large group, look for clusters of people who physically match one another. These clusters usually range from three to ten people. You'll notice that each shares behaviors such as similar postures and facial expressions. The members will even move and adjust themselves together, acting almost as a single functioning unit.

When several people are in close proximity to one another, it's natural for them to unconsciously entrain with at least one dominant person. This is especially true of groups who meet together on a regular basis. When the member or members to whom the group has entrained move to action, the others follow. *This amazing phenomenon has powerful potential for you.*

Remember: *The entrainment leader has the most influence over what is accepted or rejected by the group.* Everyone will quickly glance at this person (or persons) before determining if an idea, person, or meeting is on the right track. In effect, most group decisions are made by this person or persons. The others read their extraverbal behavior—a nod, frown, or maybe excited expression—and then act in accordance.

Whether it's your peers, superiors, or employees, remember: The group is most probably in sync with the "entrainment leader." Your job is to identify and entrain with that individual as soon as possible. *Once you have established that deep connection, the acceptance of your leadership by the group can take as little as two minutes.*

You'll be surprised at how often the entrainment leader is not the one you consider most likely. Just because the CEO, president, or member of upper management is present, don't assume the group has entrained to that individual. Even the spokesperson for the group may be getting his or her cues from someone else at the table.

When moving into unknown territory, it's best to *never assume anything.* Also, you should *constantly test your assumptions by observing the results of your actions and words on those you're leading.* Also remember: There may be two or three entrainment leaders in a group. You need to link with *each* of them prior to asserting your leadership.

When you make no connection with the entrainment leader, you run the risk of never linking with and being accepted by the group. At the beginning of any presentation, always be prepared to ask a question that necessitates an immediate answer, something like, "Would it be most useful for you to have our printed materials passed out before the presentation or after?" Or, "Do you mind if we take a few minutes and look over the agenda to be sure all the items we need covered are included?"

The answer is actually relatively meaningless. But the question initiates an interaction among the group to decide what is best for it. Watch the eye contact closely. The participants will glance most consistently at the entrainment leader. Their interaction should help you locate the leader. This allows you to begin matching him or her right from the beginning.

EXERCISE

Next time you're in a board room or staff meeting take the time to note from whom most of the group take their cue when a decision needs to be made. Be on the ball! The reactions can be subtle and quite fast. Once you know the person, that's the one you want to entrain with and address the major points of your proposals to.

In the conference room setting or other close quarters, the most effective means to entrainment is through the matching of breathing, voice tempo, posture, and gestures. When you note a feeling of connection within yourself, test the entrainment through the two-step test. When your physical changes are being followed, it's time to move on. *Because the entrainment leader follows you, the others (who already follow him or her) also accept your leadership.* This is a most elegant way of positioning yourself as a group leader without needless confrontation.

THE TIMING OF LIKABILITY

When you face groups of people it is important to remember that *each individual has a preferred speed of processing language.* This is also the person's natural speed of thinking and talking. Some people process information slowly and deliberately. Others do so at a moderate rate. There are still others whose neurology is a rapid-fire mechanism for processing language. Their brains are like computers with an accelerator board installed.

It's easy to figure out who's who. Remember: *People want to receive their information at a pace matching their speaking speed.* To generate entrainment with an entire gathering, you must give each person your information at the speed most comfortable for him or her. This means you must use the three natural language processing speeds of the individual group members. Just to make things even more interesting, you still have the talking speed and rhythm you like to use. And, unfortunately, it may not be the one most comfortable for many of those to whom you are speaking.

Why is this so important? There are few things more irritating than someone who talks too fast or too slowly for your taste. Ever listen to someone who spoke much slower than you and found yourself wanting to reach down their throat and yank the words out? Conversely, listening to a more rapid speaker can leave you feeling confused and dissatisfied. It's like making someone who never drives over 55 miles per hour speed up to 80. They're going to feel tense and out of their element. Likewise, forcing someone accustomed to driving at 65 miles per hour to slow down to 40 causes frustration. Neither is very comfortable—nor likely to feel kindly toward the person who's thrust them into this uneasy situation.

> *The rate of someone's speech is a form of communication in and of itself. To make everyone in the group comfortable, periodically match the ways each of them talks.*

In either case, after awhile the other person will usually simply stop listening, no matter how important or interesting the information may be. That's why it's crucial to pull in your listeners within the first few minutes of beginning to speak. You do this by systematically matching each of the three natural language processing speeds. The greatest orators have done this for centuries, although they probably had no idea what they were doing or why it worked so well.

We can all comfortably process language in any of the three speeds, if we are led to do so. This means *once you have matched all the group members, you may then lead them to your optimum vocal tempo or speed.* This is not only possible, but relatively simple to do.

When you first begin speaking to any group of people, you should always use a slow, deep voice. This matches up with those who are more contemplative and deliberate in their thinking. Such people characteristically process language slowly. They also speak slowly and naturally prefer to interact with those who talk the same way. You begin with them, because they can be most difficult to entrain with if initially alienated. During the first minutes of speaking, slowly present yourself and your topic. Relax. Take the time to warm up to your audience. This is like the stretching-out exercises before a run.

You will identify the slow processors immediately. They will be those obviously most comfortable with your presentation. They will be content, because you're speaking in the manner most satisfactory to them. Those people exhibiting a moderate comfort level are the ones with a moderate language processing speed. They like receiving information from someone speaking in a moderate tempo and using a modulated, balanced tone.

Within the first four to five minutes, you'll notice some people beginning to fidget and become restless. These uncomfortable individuals are probably those who like to receive information rapidly and constantly, favoring a fast-paced presentation. Don't worry about their initial discomfort. You'll be gathering them in soon.

Once you have matched the slower speakers for five to seven minutes more, begin to pick up the pace of your delivery. This will gently lead the slower speakers to a medium tempo. It will also begin to match those preferring a more moderate pace. *After five to seven minutes, pick up the pace again. This accommodates those who enjoy the fast speed.* You will then have matched the entire group. *You can now lead everyone to the tone and tempo with which you are most comfortable.* They will naturally and comfortably follow your lead.

EXERCISE

Next time you have a speech to give take the first minutes to use this technique. The times listed are a good rule of thumb.

The steps are:
Slow-speaking speed for 3 to 7 minutes.
Moderate-speaking speed for 3 to 7 minutes.
Fast-speaking speed for 3 to 7 minutes.
Lead the entire group to your preferred level.

This technique is useful in preventing the alienation of listeners. Its weak point: When the process is used alone it takes fifteen to twenty minutes. If you use additional techniques while speaking, you can speed things up considerably.

What you choose to speak about and how you use movement can make all the difference. Following are some important tools you will be using to create entrainment with large groups of people. By layering and combining a few of these at the beginning of your presentation or meeting, you can reduce the time for the process to about five minutes. .

THE STRATEGY THAT ENSURES OTHERS WILL FOLLOW

When facing a group, you have two options for generating entrainment. One is syncing and matching the behavior and thinking of the individuals. The second is to have everyone match or sync with you. Although either can be successful, *having the group match you is the faster and more efficient method.*

The first step is aligning the group. This is meant literally. *You want everyone in the group to gradually align physically until they match with you.* In short order, this can develop strong entrainment and form a sense of community. You may then comfortably lead the group in the direction you desire.

Of the many methods for getting people to match and align with you, one technique is used often because it's amazingly simple. All you need do is ask questions so basic or general that all the people raise their hands in positive response. We've all heard speakers ask questions such as

"How many of you would like to make more money than you do now?" (The speaker raises his hand and, not surprisingly, so do most audience members.)

"How many of you would like to move into a nicer home with the same monthly payments you now have?" (The speaker raises her hand. Guess what—audience members do too.)

"How many of you would like to double your income in the next six months?" (The speaker raises his hand and . . .)

Why do speakers ask such obviously leading questions? Of course, they want to generate interest in and excitement for their topic. They most certainly want to draw in their listeners. But, most important, they are developing a basic level of synchrony.

When you ask questions that people will certainly answer in the affirmative, and *have them respond by raising their hands* just like *you, you are guiding them toward making a connection with you.* As people follow and respond to your questions, they become more and more conditioned to follow you. To do what you ask. To become aligned with you.

EXERCISE

Whenever you have a presentation to deliver have at least five to seven simple alignment questions ready to go. Consider them your secret weapons for success. Even if you don't intend to use them, they're great to have ready to soothe even the most difficult audience.

Physical and Mental Alignment

Physical and mental alignment can take place in a number of ways. A number of motivational speakers start their presentations by having the audience stand and follow them in exercises. They stretch one way. Audience members stretch with them. Then they stretch the other way. People move with them again and again. At the end of the exercise, they ask people to sit down. They do. The audience has begun to become aligned with the speaker even before he or she begins the presentation. They are becoming accustomed to following the speaker's directions.

The Reverend Jesse Jackson is a master of this technique. Within minutes, he aligns groups, bringing them into synchrony. You may recall seeing televised excerpts of occasions like a large youth conference where Jackson initiated the "I am somebody!" phrase. It became a rallying cry of the black pride movement.

Jackson first divided the audience into sections. He led one to repeat the words, "I am!" and the next to shout, "Somebody!" He began a competition among the groups, encouraging them to outshout the others. He repeatedly urged each group to be louder and more enthusiastic than the others. Soon everyone was following his lead. He had complete control of what could have been a challenging audience. Members became a cohesive group conditioned to follow Jackson's lead. He accomplished all this in a way that was entertaining for audience members.

You are limited only by your imagination when you use this technique to develop synchrony with and leadership over a group. *Giving group members simple tasks quickly accustoms them to following your directions.* The task can be as elementary as introducing yourself then asking each member to introduce himself to the person behind him. You might ask audience members to write notes at specific times or select a partner for later assignments. Aside from the possibility of building community, these tasks have little concrete value. But they do begin the process of conditioning the audience to follow your directions, your lead.

There is another good reason for beginning a presentation with a request to perform simple tasks. It short-circuits the people (and many groups have them) who are prepared to not comply with any requests. It's difficult for even the most troublesome people to not follow such simple directions. They would be hard pressed to provide a sound reason for their recalcitrance, thus appearing unreasonable.

The skilled leader goes on to provide larger and more concrete tasks. *The group will continue to follow directions if the leader methodically builds its willingness to do so.* There are sales presentations where the audience is given a number of simple things to do. The tasks are slowly made more substantial until finally members are asked to buy the product. When these techniques are used in a methodical manner, many more people are receptive to purchasing the product than would have been otherwise.

If we are patient and methodical, groups will fol-
low virtually any ethical lead as long as they have
been gradually conditioned to comply with ever-
expanding directions.

The techniques of mental alignment work just as well in virtually all settings. A lawyer begins syncing the jury by using *simple and obviously true statements* such as, "As you've been sitting here listening, trying to decide what to believe and what not to believe, you have developed a feeling for who has and who hasn't been telling the truth." Everyone concurs with this. They *have* been sitting, listening, and trying to decide what to believe. And most probably they *have* formulated feelings for who has and who hasn't been truthful.

Then the lawyer says, "Believe me when I say that I came into court today prepared to convince you of my client's innocence." Once again, people nod their heads. That's easy to believe. A perceptive lawyer will continue to layer these kinds of statements until the jury becomes conditioned to believe whatever is being said.

By trial's close, the jury has been given so many easy-to-believe statements it is conditioned to believe the attorney. The attorney can now lead members when making stronger statements to direct their thoughts, such as, "And we know that the prosecution's witnesses all lacked credibility." Thus, the jury follows the lead of the defense attorney who so skillfully matched it to gain ultimate entrainment.

In the same vein, when strong leaders come into new jobs they often begin interacting with their employees by asking simple questions and assigning uncomplicated tasks.

Would you mind getting me the budget files?

Could you show me to the coffee room?

Could you run this over to the main office for me?

The new manager has few problems assuming leadership as each employee becomes accustomed to follow directions.

> **EXERCISE**
>
> **Come up with three alignment techniques for each category that you can use tomorrow at work. Be creative!**
>
> - **Alignment questions**
> - **Physical movement**
> - **Simple tasks**
> - **Simple and obvious statements**

Learning to creatively align a group in any situation may take a little thought on your part. *Remember, the greater amount of physical movement the audience follows you through, the better.* It's helpful to watch a variety of motivational speakers and even televangelists. These people lead groups of thousands and keep them coming back week after week. Many of them are masters of mass communication, both verbal and extraverbal. Watch and analyze them every chance you get. Write down every new technique you learn for future use.

HOW TO ENTRAIN PEOPLE TO YOUR LEADERSHIP

Those who say they have "no rhythm" are absolutely wrong. People are naturally rhythmic animals moving harmoniously through life. Our heartbeat, our walking gait, our breathing, and the tempo of our speech all fall into rhythmic patterns.

A basketball player making a fast break down the court or a sales manager speaking to his sales team are each moving and communicating in accordance with unique rhythms. *Developing a distinct rhythm with others creates a powerful unconscious bond people are unwilling to break.* Once in the dance of synchrony, people are reluctant for it to end. Breaking synchrony feels as discordant as trying to do the two-step while your partner is doing the waltz. *Creating a group rhythm is an excellent way to generate entrainment.*

Rhythmic Alignment

Rhythmic alignment may sound difficult to create, but in application it's quite easy. *The important thing to know is that people naturally entrain to the most distinctive and dominant rhythm in their environment.* We seem to naturally, far outside of consciousness, be drawn to the distinctive and strong rhythms around us. Without knowing it, our minds identify them and move us into synchrony with them.

During a corporate training we observed, the trainers played at low volume a tape consisting simply of a bass rhythm and drums. The trainers spoke in rhythm with the music. It wasn't long before the group was entrained, either swaying or tapping a foot or pencils to the beat. The effect was so pervasive that people began walking and asking questions in time to the music. This created a sense of community, allowing the trainers to lead easily.

Creating group alignment and leadership acceptance with music can work even with larger groups in less controlled situations. As an entertainment director on a large cruise ship in the Caribbean, I had the unique challenge of using three staff members to coordinate 700 to 1,200 passengers. Disembarking for sightseeing or shopping tours, the passengers would be anxious to get to their respective buses. At some point, they'd be spread out between the ship's deck, on tender boats shuttling back and forth between ship and island, and on the island itself.

Should any of the hundreds of excited and rambunctious people miss their slated tours, we had to reconnect them to it later in the day. This meant less free time for us. We were motivated to get the group working together and on their respective ways.

The remedy turned out to be quite simple. We had members of the ship's reggae band come up with a tune that

was easy to sing along with and included lots of hand gestures. From the stage, we'd ask the passengers questions that
got them to raise their hands and answer in unison. Next, we
had them get into specific lines according to "rules" we
devised. People grew accustomed to following our directions. While still on stage, we taught them the song and
movements to go with it. Soon, all 700 to 1,200 people were
happily following us in perfect unison.

The catchy tune made it easy and fun to continue, hand
gestures and all, on the tender boats. By the time we all
landed on the island, we had a large group of people moving
in total synchrony. The three staff members could easily
direct passengers to their respective destinations. Few ever
missed their ride.

Another way to align a group rhythmically is to adjust
its breathing pattern to yours. As strange as this might sound,
it's done all the time. Have you ever seen a comedian's live
performance or been in a group where someone entertained
with funny stories? Did it feel good to laugh with others? As
you listened and laughed did you begin to feel more relaxed
and comfortable with those around you? After awhile, did
you feel more a part of the group? Probably so.

As people laugh they fall into synchronized and rhythmic breathing. This happens because we normally laugh only
while exhaling. If we laugh at the same time (at punch lines)
we exhale at the same time. We then inhale together. After
only a few jokes, breathing rates are synchronized and a
strong linkage has been established between the audience
and the performer. Films of this phenomenon are striking.

A Bill Cosby skit underscores in a humorous fashion
breathing as a technique for creating entrainment. Cosby
recounts how when he was a boy his father snored so loud
the whole house shook (a distinctive and dominant rhythm).
The snoring was so pervasive it dominated the house, forcing
everybody else to breathe with him. This created a problem
when, every once in a while, his dad skipped a breath. Then,
as Cosby tells it, he and his brother would sit up in bed and
yell, "Dad! Breathe so we can breathe!" Cosby's skit reveals

once again the phenomenon of how, once entrained, people function in synchrony.

Singing accomplishes the same thing. Think about a time you sang with others in church, school, a party, or another event. Whenever a group of people sing together, they quickly fall into unconscious synchrony. *Syncing actually occurs whenever people make any continuous set of motions at the same time.* For example, at church services people not only sing together. They also sit, stand, and kneel at the same time. They spend much time functioning as a single synchronized unit under the direction of the clergy. This is one reason church members create a strong bond among themselves.

Now think back to a time you watched a serious movie at a theater. As the movie progressed, you probably did not grow more comfortable with the people around you. In all likelihood you never felt the audience was a group of which you were a part. You probably walked out as isolated from the others as you were when you walked in. That's because most movies do not attempt to create any level of group synchrony in the audience. Their goal is not to create community but to entertain, provide escape.

BECOMING THE HEART OF SUCCESS

No matter their differences, virtually every great charismatic figure we've studied has entrained listeners using the same dynamic technique. They all create powerful entrainment through the rhythmic use of their voices. In essence, *they use their voices to communicate at two levels, both with words and with rhythm.*

Of course, they were quite elegant with their words. But, they also created a highly distinctive and definable rhythm with their voice. They became the most distinctive and dominant rhythm in their environment. Their vocal quality drew people closer and closer to their leadership. It was a language in and of itself with its own meaning and form. *All charismatic leaders synchronize and intensify the ever-present rhythms of human interactions to strengthen their connection with those listening.*

We are fortunate. The basic linguistic structure of English offers us many possibilities for establishing a dynamic speaking rhythm. Other languages, such as French or Italian, have a more natural "singsong" quality, a built-in rhythm of sorts. The structure of English, however, accommodates itself to the natural speaking rhythm of the user.

> *People will naturally entrain to the most distinctive and dominant rhythm in their environment. If you become that element, you will forever have the gift of drawing people close.*

This means that, when spoken, the rhythm of the English language is unique to the *user* rather than being inherent in the language itself. With English, it's up to us whether we speak in a droning, dragging rhythm or use a dynamic, engaging one. Unfortunately, because it's so easy to speak in a flat manner, far too many people do. That's why *those who spice up their speaking rhythm with dynamic intonation patterns, intensity, and varied tempos stand far out in front of the crowd.*

Each of us speaks with our own basic rhythm driven by other, more complex internal rhythms. To capture the interest of others and fully engage their mental processes, you must go beyond the metronome voice you hear all too often. Remember, *people will entrain with the most dominant and distinct rhythm in their environment*. Make your voice come alive with a rhythm that includes changes in tempo, intonation, and intensity. *You will then become that most dominant and distinctive rhythm.* You will also communicate the emotion so important to charismatic communication.

There are two ways to entrain others with your voice. The first is through the length of your spoken phrases or the structure of your speech. The second is by creating a rhythmically dynamic vocal quality through the use of tempo, pitch intonation, and intensity. The best charismatic leaders use a combination of both.

Entrainment Through Speech Structure

The structure of your speech can have an entraining effect. When speaking in a strong, rhythmic fashion you create a succession of similar syllables and pauses. The length of the sentences or phrases you utter, when similar in duration and accentuated by slight pauses, will produce entrainment as a natural by-product.

A speech by Winston Churchill demonstrates this wonderfully.

> We shall not flag or fail.
> We shall go on to the end. (pause)
> We shall fight in France.
> We shall fight on the seas and oceans. (pause)
> We shall fight with growing confidence and growing strength in the air.
> We shall defend our island, whatever the cost may be. (pause)
> We shall fight on the beaches.
> We shall fight on the landing grounds. (pause)
> We shall fight in the fields and in the streets.
> We shall fight in the hills. (pause)
> We shall never surrender.

By the very structure of his speech, the number of words per phrase, the number of syllables per phrase, a very profound and distinctive rhythm is created. The length of each distinctive segment should be fairly short and of consistent length to ensure the dominance of the rhythmic effect. Just by continuing on with such a rhythm you will draw your audience in toward you. Listen to any speech by John F. Kennedy for a perfect example of entrainment through speech structure.

Vocal Quality

Where you choose to accent or stress the syllables of words, along with how you alternate them with unstressed syllables, produces the rhythm of your speech (Brown, 1991).

We've all heard people who had so much trouble reading out loud it was painful listening to them. Their voice was void of tonal variation (intonation), and they pronounced words slowly, syllable by syllable. We didn't listen to what they read for very long. It was too difficult. We became bored and were easily distracted. We soon turned our attention to something else. The same happens when we speak to people.

To entrain large groups of people with your voice, you must consider qualities of your voice such as speech tempo. It should be varied to match the emotional interest you have in the point you're making. Let's say the basic rhythm of your normal speech is four beats per measure. When you talk about something exciting, your speech should become more rapid, going up to sixteen beats per measure. If you were expressing sadness, you'd slow down to two beats per measure. In each case, you maintain the *rhythm* of your speech, you just vary the *tempo*.

There are a number of different qualities to our voices that, when used in conjunction with one another, can create an entraining effect. The four most prominent are:

TEMPO: The rate of speed we speak or, most important, the changes in the rate of speed.

PITCH: The highness or lowness of the voice on the musical scale.

INTONATION: The highs and lows of the voice's pitch as it occurs along the speech chain.

INTENSITY: The voice's loudness or volume used to mark out emotionally emphasized points.

As we've demonstrated, you can create your distinct rhythm of speech using the natural break of the words' syllables. This, however, limits you to short, choppy sentences that carry the beat for you. But you have options. You can create a strong rhythmic effect by creating periodic fluctuations in the tempo, pitch, intonation, or intensity of your voice. This creates the same effect, but by using variations in your vocal quality. In this way you can rhythmically break up longer sentences with stresses placed on certain words. Think of the singsong voice of many televangelists. Although most use this technique to an extreme, it is an excellent example of this ability.

For example, you can speak in sentences comprising five beats per phrase (as in the previous section) or instead use long sentences in which you place tonal emphasis on the fifth beat or syllable of your sentence. You may create your rhythmic pattern by stressing every second, third, fourth, or fifth beat. It's up to you. The only criterion is the creation of sufficient rhythm to which people can entrain.

EXERCISE

Since it's difficult to translate sounds into the written word, take a few minutes to learn from the best. Listen to the powerfully rhythmic voices of the following people:

- **John F. Kennedy**
- **Ronald Reagan**
- **Winston Churchill**
- **Martin Luther King, Jr.**
- **Jesse Jackson**
- **Any major televangelist**

HARNESSING YOUR GREATEST ALLY

When you know and acknowledge the pervasive beliefs and values of others, you can quickly generate a powerful bond. You don't have to personally hold the beliefs or values. All you need do is structure your meeting or presentation to take the others' view of reality into account.

We used this technique successfully during a presentation to a group of veteran intelligence agents in Washington, D.C. As we had lunch with the group's branch manager the day before the presentation, he related some disturbing news. The manager said a previous training with another company had gone poorly. Therefore, the agents resented this program sight unseen. In fact, the manager said, some of them intended to challenge and disrupt the presentation.

When we returned to the headquarters after lunch, a discussion with many of the agents who would attend the presentation turned up several beliefs and values. We listened once again for strong statements beginning with words such as "people are . . .," "life is . . .," and "I will . . . ." Beliefs are often verbalized this way. By the end of the day, eight beliefs that seemed universal among the agents had been identified.

During the first five minutes of the presentation we mentioned each belief and value uncovered along with how they fit in with our program. Note, they were "mentioned," not claimed as ours. There was simple acknowledgment of the agents' perceptions of the world.

The agents learned how their beliefs fit in with the program. This developed a bond with the entire group, even with those who had previously been most hostile. The path was now clear for entrainment to occur naturally. There was no attempt to disrupt the program. The training was a re-sounding success.

Matching beliefs and values is a crucial element for entraining with individuals and groups. Charismatic politicians are excellent at this. John F. Kennedy, Ronald Reagan, and Jesse Jackson each exhibited charisma, influencing people to take action. Because each expounded on different values during his speeches, he connected with different segments of the population.

THE SIMPLICITY OF BONDING
WITH A NATION

Every great leader must have the ability to bring groups of people together so they function as a single, coordinated body dedicated to success. The group's acceptance of the leader is essential to that outcome. Matching experience is a subtle and simple technique for gaining acceptance. It's used successfully by many charismatic leaders.

Matching experience is the art of getting into your group members' minds and matching their perceptions of the world. It is, quite simply, talking about those things they are experiencing or have experienced. You then share with them what they have been living. It *validates* not only what people experience but what they think and feel.

More important, by validating things that people are thinking about, have experienced, or have felt, you begin to create an agreeable atmosphere. They begin a habit of agreeing with you because you are telling them things with which they cannot disagree.

When used consistently, this technique creates an atmosphere of mutuality and agreement. This is the best atmosphere in which to present your ideas. It can substantially ease potential opposition, particularly the "knee-jerk" kind with which some people greet any and all new concepts.

All leaders must at some time address negative emotions and issues. At the same time, they must be careful not to perpetuate the negativity. As President Franklin D. Roosevelt obviously knew, *recognizing and acknowledging the fear, then offering hope is the best way to solve this leadership dilemma.*

During the Great Depression, Roosevelt identified the first enemy American citizens had to defeat before moving forward. This was the fear that had brought the nation to its knees. People had watched their economic system crash and their safeguards fail. They faced unemployment that respected neither skill, experience, nor desire to work. They stood in food lines and went home to houses they couldn't afford to heat or light.

Everywhere they turned, people were assaulted with increasingly harsher reality. There was no safety. Everything they had depended upon had failed them. Fear and anxiety were the constant companions of even the most able citizens of this nation. It's no wonder they created images of a future even bleaker than the dreary present in which they struggled to survive.

Roosevelt neither denied nor disparaged the fear of those he led. He didn't attempt to coat dark reality with a whitewash of optimism. Instead, he faced head-on what was on the mind of every American.

> So, first of all, let me assert my firm belief that the only thing we have to fear is fear itself: nameless, unreasoning, unjustified terror which paralyzes needed efforts to convert retreat into advance.

Roosevelt didn't *tell* people he knew they were afraid or that he knew how they felt. He didn't dwell on fear or attempt to make it less in anyone's mind. He simply recognized it. Fear was a reality that could not be denied. Yet there was a real danger of increasing it by talking about it.

So, Roosevelt made a connection with his listeners by speaking about the fear that gnawed at their insides. He did what they couldn't: looked fear straight in the eye and didn't blink. He neither condemned those who were afraid nor fed their fear. He named it and described it. He showed that he *knew* and *understood* what they felt.

Another example of matching experience is the persuasive testimony of Colonel Oliver North during the 1987 Congressional Select Committee hearings on the Iran-Contra affair. There's no doubt that during those hearings, North communicated charismatically.

For almost a year, North had been the subject of countless newspaper and magazine articles and television reports. Previously, few people had been aware of the mysterious colonel who had worked out of the White House "Basement." But during the year preceding the hearings, the nation had been inundated with convincing commentary. There had been a national perception created of North as the perpetrator of worldwide, cloak-and-dagger crimes.

For the people of this nation, judgment was in long before North rose to speak on his own behalf. It didn't seem to be a question of "Is he guilty?" but of "How guilty is he?" Yet, once North spoke on his own behalf, much of the nation began heralding "Ollie the Hero." Cries of "Ollie for President" were heard. Overnight he became a national folk hero.

What did Colonel North do when he began his testimony that morning of July 9, 1987, to so drastically change a national perception? He began his statement to the committee with, and continued to use statements that were simple, straightforward, and couldn't be denied by any rational person. The things of which he spoke were either actually being witnessed by viewers as he spoke or had been witnessed by them over the past year. He didn't speak of one thing that anyone watching and listening could say, "That is not true."

North bonded with a watching nation. He began by saying: "My best friend is my wife Betsy to whom I have been married for 19 years and with whom I have had four wonderful children, aged 18, 16, 11, and 6." As viewers watched on television, they could see his wife sitting behind him. She obviously agreed with and supported him. He obviously told the truth about his marriage and children.

No matter what they might be thinking, the unconscious minds of listeners could feel at ease with this man so far. Next he said: "I came to the National Security Council six years ago to work in the administration of a great president." That too was true. He *had* been at the Council for six years.

As he continued to speak, *North layered simple truth upon simple truth.* These statements further calmed conscious minds. Although some listeners may have wondered why he was talking about who his best friend was, they certainly couldn't feel North was lying.

Later in the testimony, North said (emphasis is ours):

I would not be frank with you if I did not admit that the last several months *have been difficult for* me and *my family*. It has been *difficult to be* on the front pages of every newspaper in the land *day after day*, to be the lead story on national television *day after day, to be* photographed thousands of times by bands of photographers who *chased* us around since November *just because* my name arose in the hearings. *It is difficult to be caught in the middle* of a constitutional struggle between the executive and legislative branches over who will formulate and direct the foreign policy of this nation. (North, 1987)

Who could deny any of this? The listeners' minds had to agree with virtually everything in this statement. After all, most aware Americans had either seen North in the newspapers or on television during the past year. They recalled the scenes of reporters chasing him. Even those who hadn't knew that anyone in the same situation would find those things unbearably difficult to live with.

Notice the previous italicized words (added by the authors) and the message they deliver. Although what North had been involved in appeared light years away from the day-to-day experiences of most Americans, he expressed himself in terms of the very human feelings involved. The words "difficult for my family," "difficult to be day after day," "day after day to be," "chased, just because," "It is difficult to be caught in the middle."

Who hasn't been in situations difficult for their families? Where it (whatever "it" was) was difficult day after day? We all know that sometimes the hardest thing of all is "day after day to be." Who hasn't been "chased" in some fashion "just because" of something that occurred by happenstance? And, finally, is there anyone alive who doesn't know the terrible feeling of being caught in the middle? There was no way anyone could deny what North was saying. They could also empathize with him. Slowly, we began to lean toward believing everything he said. We did so because in this cluttered and complex world he spoke simply and directly.

Further, during his testimony, North embodied all the internal qualities in Section One. Even those who disliked him or disagreed with his actions couldn't deny that he had done what he believed to be right. *He had direction and optimistically expressed it.* Second, *he had a passion for his career, accomplishments, and country. He was completely dedicated to his job and his country.* Third, *he was totally congruent.*

North had lost his cherished job in the White House, been hounded by the press for almost a year, and been called before the Select Committee. There he sat, in front of committee members, newspaper and television reporters, and a watching world. He never flinched or wavered. He remained loyal to the beliefs and values he testified had brought him there. *Because he possessed the necessary internal qualities, North was able to develop entrainment with most of the country.* His values matched ours. He accomplished this in many of the ways outlined in Chapters 2 and 3. But *the most striking technique was how he matched our experience of what we saw and heard.*

EXERCISE

Especially during business dealings and presentations we've been taught to speak in lofty platitudes, to pull out our mental thesaurus and dictionary to make sure everyone believes we're competent. We've been taught that the greater the vocabulary, the greater the intelligence.

THROW THAT TRAINING AWAY!
The most powerful leaders use the down-home, straightforward approach. Your listeners appreciate it, believe you more, and most important, it has a sizzling effect on people!

Give it a try.

KEEPING THEM ON THE EDGE OF THEIR SEATS

Keeping people on the edge on their seats is another excellent way to maintain solid control and deepen entrainment. Unfortunately, few topics lend themselves to generating that kind of intense interest. There is, however, a subtle technique that's been used by expert storytellers for generations. You can use it to maintain interest throughout a presentation. It's called opening and closing stories.

Open stories are a way of preventing your audience from prematurely coming to your conclusion and then loosing interest. This situation, called closure, can be avoided by breaking up a story and telling the first half to two-thirds early on in a presentation and then saving the end for the end of the presentation. Without the whole story, the mind lacks understanding and therefore continues to search through your words for meaning. In this way an open story(s) creates a small amount of stress while the mind searches for understanding and therefore closure.

With open stories, our mind isn't given enough information to get "the whole picture." Can you remember overhearing a conversation that was really interesting? One where you heard something you couldn't quite believe was true. It was fascinating, intriguing, or exciting. Then, just as the person came to the most important part, he began to whisper or walked away and you didn't hear the rest of it. How long did you keep thinking about it?

Skilled leaders use open stories often to subtly keep the group's interest. To do these, start a story early in your presentation. Once the group is interested in hearing the end, move on to another subject. People will listen intently for the outcome. This is referred to as "opening the story."

The strategy is to open one or more stories. Once you have generated interest, give the group the important information you want them to have; they will listen intently. After your done close the stories. With this technique, you dramatically reduce the chance that people will close their mind to your message or miss it due to daydreaming or other distractions. You open the minds of your group, drop in the important information and then allow the group to come to closure by completing the stories. *By opening stories, you can get people to intently listen to the important information you want them to have.*

> *A leader using open stories is like the oyster farmer prying open an oyster to drop in a grain of sand. If the grain is planted correctly, the oyster will use it to develop a pearl.*

Open stories are probably the most effective way to keep a group interested and waiting to hear more. Once the story is 60 to 80 percent complete, switch to another subject or story. The more abrupt the change the better. Forget about transitions. Just switch to another subject. *Since this isn't a normal or comfortable way for us to communicate, be sure to practice open stories fully. Also, be sure you close them once you have delivered your information, if you don't, people will go away with an uneasy feeling.*

A good way to structure these is to have several interesting stories. Open each of them to create interest in what you're saying, then close them in the reverse order.

For example:

```
┌────────  Story 1 Open
│ ┌──────  Story 2 Open
│ │ ┌────  Story 3 Open
│ │ │ ┌──  Story 4 Open
│ │ │ │       Discuss subject matter
│ │ │ └──  Story 4 Close
│ │ └────  Story 3 Close
│ └──────  Story 2 Close
└────────  Story 1 Close
```

In Short

1. The same principles that allow you to entrain with one other person are applicable with groups, from small to large.

2. When leading small groups of people you can methodically sync with or match one person at a time until the group comfortably falls under your leadership.

3. Larger groups of people require a variety of other powerful techniques to create alignment. Alignment techniques work in much the same way. They match an individual and eventually lead him or her toward entrainment. Alignment isn't a direct route. By applying it a number of times, however, you can draw virtually any size group comfortably under your leadership. These techniques fall under three categories:

   PHYSICAL ALIGNMENT

   MENTAL ALIGNMENT

   RHYTHMIC ALIGNMENT

4. People will entrain to the most distinctive and dominant rhythm in their environment. Become that element and people will naturally draw toward you.

5. The entrainment technique most used by great charismatic leaders is vocal entrainment. It employs the elements of the voice to create an exciting and enticing charismatic persona.

THE CHARISMA FACTOR

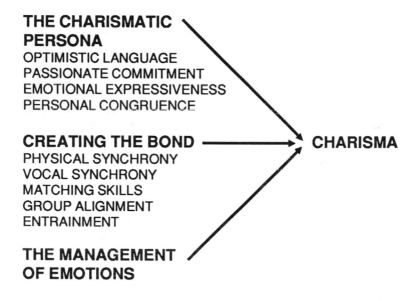

**THE CHARISMATIC
PERSONA**
OPTIMISTIC LANGUAGE
PASSIONATE COMMITMENT
EMOTIONAL EXPRESSIVENESS
PERSONAL CONGRUENCE

CREATING THE BOND ⟶ **CHARISMA**
PHYSICAL SYNCHRONY
VOCAL SYNCHRONY
MATCHING SKILLS
GROUP ALIGNMENT
ENTRAINMENT

**THE MANAGEMENT
OF EMOTIONS**

Generating The Power of Charisma

7

EMOTIONAL MANAGEMENT: THE HEART OF CHARISMA

Leaders with charisma do more than provide direction. They *inspire* others. They elegantly harness the strongest and most productive emotions that are the fuel of human performance and excellence. In return, others are not mere supporters following orders. They seize the charismatic leaders' direction and share their dreams.

As a charismatic leader *you can direct the thoughts of others, guiding them to the source of their best efforts.* Bypassing logical communication, *you can focus thoughts by generating within people the necessary emotional responses.* This guides them to the source of their own best efforts.

While others focus on managing people, the charismatic leader is managing emotions. This is far simpler than it sounds. In this chapter, you will learn techniques used by great charismatic communicators. Techniques used today are no different from those used hundreds of years ago. There's really only one difference: We now recognize and understand what previously was done by instinct.

EMOTIONAL MANAGEMENT: THE KEY TO INSPIRING ACTION

Sometimes, no matter how hard you try, you just can't *make* people take the action you want. You try to get customers to buy, citizens to vote, employees to become part of the team, or prospects to donate, with no luck. You envy those able to create in others the *desire* to walk with them down the path they've chosen. How do they do it?

Because human beings are emotionally driven creatures, *feeling always precedes action*. People *must* be in the appropriate emotional state of mind before they *want* to do something. They must somehow *feel* like doing it before they willingly do it.

When we

. . . *feel* hungry we eat.

. . . *feel* passionate, we make love.

. . . *feel* curious, we seek learning.

. . . *feel* the need for something, we buy it.

. . . *feel* they are honest, we support them.

Using emotional management, you activate the minds of those listening to you. Emotions become paths down which you draw others to their destination. Customers feel intrigued, fascinated, delighted, and motivated. Or voters feel inspired, impressed, and trusting. Or employees feel secure, needed, and valued.

> *All charismatic leaders know their most valuable resources are the emotions they generate in others. They take their listeners on a roller coaster ride of emotion that ends with the task at hand.*

When the necessary emotions are surging through them employees, clients, constituents, or donors naturally want to jump in and make things happen—often before you ask. *Think what you could accomplish if you were able to instill in others the emotions and feelings they need to perform at their peak.*

Imagine kicking off a difficult project and inspiring in frightened and uncertain employees the confidence that fuels an outstanding performance. Imagine dealing with hesitant clients and eliciting a desire in them that makes your product prized. Consider what would happen if, when constituents became disillusioned, you were able to inspire hope that assured their continued support. Or when donors were apathetic about a cause, you could generate empathy and compassion that turned to enthusiastic support.

The standard method for getting people to do what you want is to ask, providing what seems to be the most motivating reasons for your request. If you are like most people, these reasons appeal in large part to logic and reason. There's a problem with this. *Due to the number of variables involved, you can't predict how others' minds will process the information you give them.* Whether they will or will not comply with your request depends on many things. These include the nature or cost of the request, whether what's important to you is important to them, how the others feel toward you, your relative status with them, and so on.

With entrainment, however, you move past extraneous considerations. You begin dealing with communication techniques that stimulate both sides of the brain and, invariably, the person. *As a charismatic leader you generate the emotional desire in people, then show them the road you wish to travel with them.* Even the most difficult employees, clients, or voters may find themselves eagerly turning down a new pathway.

It's important to remember that people have all sorts of emotions within them. Your job is to go in and pull up the right ones. Normally, this would seem to be about as easy as groping around a dark hole among hundreds of identically shaped objects to find a specific one. However, using the tools of emotional management—the same tools used by charismatic leaders for centuries—it becomes a straightforward process.

The techniques of emotional management weave a picture in the minds of those around you. This picture can create an emotional impact. Since emotions are your primary resource, it doesn't matter so much what you say as long as it creates the appropriate emotions. This is why you can be touched by charismatic communicators and later wonder what it was they really said.

Presidents Ronald Reagan and John F. Kennedy were experts at emotional management. Within minutes they had touched listeners' hearts. Later analysis would often show no definitive content to their speeches. In a speech conferring honorary citizenship on Winston Churchill, Kennedy made a statement revealing his understanding of the power of charismatic communication.

HOW DO YOU CREATE A PRESIDENTIAL SPEECH TODAY?

Since the enormous power and popularity of Ronald Reagan, the standard for presidential media presence has been forever heightened. Because of his ability to consistently touch the heartstrings of the American citizen we no longer are happy with a good administrator, a good leader. We want a leader who can *move* us.

Technology has now taken a great deal of the guesswork out of the process. Today, a speech can be practiced on videotape and shown to focus groups equipped with "people meters." These are devices supplied to each member of the focus group, which allow them to continuously rate the emotional impact of the speech by turning the dial from low to high.

The data from the group is funnelled through a computer, and the results are later superimposed over the speaker's face on the TV. This allows the consultants, handlers, and speech writers to know precisely which parts of the presentation are having a powerful impact and which parts aren't. The final speech can then be crafted and honed to have a specific impact prior to giving it to the general public.

In the dark days and darker nights when England stood alone—and most men save Englishmen despaired of England's life—he mobilized the English language and sent it into battle. The incandescent quality of his words illuminated the courage of his countrymen.

IDEODYNAMIC RESPONSE: THE SECRET OF CHARISMA

Ido = Idea and Dynamic = Action
IDEAS TO ACTION

Emotional management works thanks to a process within each of us called the ideodynamic response. This is when feelings and emotions well up inside as we think of certain things. When we recall a particular person or experience, the set of emotions linked to them *naturally* begins to course through our body.

When we mentally focus on something the connected emotional response rises up with it. We can't help it. Think about a time you got together with friends and told a story from the past. It might have been of a youthful prank, a military experience, a camping trip, serious illness of a loved one, or a grueling project at work.

In order to tell the story, you had to replay the event. As you saw it in your mind and described it to your friends, you were virtually reliving it. This was followed by actual reexperiencing of the connected emotions. You were happy, frightened, excited, angry, sad, resourceful, or proud all over again. Depending upon your ability as a storyteller, the potency of the event, and the level of entrainment, others may have become as caught up in the emotions as you were—even if they weren't anywhere around when the event actually occurred. This is the ideodynamic response at work.

Thoughts are always associated with subtle and not-so-subtle emotional feelings. That's because within the brain the areas mediating thoughts and feelings are intricately interconnected. In fact, it's almost impossible to have a thought without at the same time having some feeling about it. On some occasions, the feelings are as evanescent and subtle as sunlight playing on gently moving water. But with some practice it's possible to be swift enough to tune in to these feelings. Often they take the form of bodily sensations: a vague sense of "heaviness" somewhere in the chest or legs or head, migraine headaches, a problem with getting one's breath, and so on [emphasis added]. (Restak, 1991)

How many times have you asked people about something important to them, maybe their hobby, children, profession, or political stance. Almost instantly you could see and hear a significant change in their physiologies. Their eyes got wide and bright. They might have begun talking faster and even louder. They might have leaned toward you.

What happened is that by the simple asking of a question you set off a literal barrage of emotions within these people. With just a few words you focused their thoughts on memories and experiences rich in powerful feelings.

Neurologists believe a small, almond-shaped nucleus in the limbic system of the brain called the amygdala is responsible for this phenomenon. The amygdala takes the glut of information that bombards us constantly and somehow ties together selected experiences with certain emotions. This gives an emotional meaning to the event. *These experiences are encoded into the brain with whatever positive or negative emotions have been tied to them.* This creates the foundation of our personality and memory.

Prior to these discoveries, charismatic communicators couldn't know what they were doing or how they were doing it. Still, by talking about things that naturally sent emotions surging through others, they have always made good use of the ideodynamic response.

As we listen to someone speaking, our minds go through a variety of processes in order to understand what is being said. There are no dictionaries floating around in our brain mass listing words and definitions. *To our brain, words alone are no more than familiar sounds, having no meaning in and of themselves.* What we do have is an extensive series of memories and experiences from our past. It is from these experiences that we learn the meaning we attach to a given word.

When a word enters our ear as a sound, it is transformed into a neurological impulse. Our mind searches for the meaning it has attached to that particular impulse. For example, the word *comfort* has no more meaning than any other utterance unless somewhere along the line we associated it with a certain kind of experience.

Let's say that one day when you were a child you were lying on the couch, pillow under your head, watching television and eating potato chips. Someone walked by and said, "Boy, you look comfortable." It was then that the word comfort had meaning for you, because there was now an experience associated with it.

From that time on, if you were asked to think about being comfortable you would see yourself lying on the couch, hear the sounds of the television, taste the salty crunchiness of the potato chips, and feel the softness of the pillow under your head. With that image would come that special feeling your mind identifies as "comfort." If someone asked you right now to think of being comfortable, what it means to you, what image does it evoke?

When someone speaks, we have to make thousands of internal representations of what is being said. It's the mind's way of interpreting words into its own language, which consists of pictures, sounds, and feelings.

EXERCISE

Think for a moment about each of the following questions and notice the ideodynamic response in action.

• Where did you have your first real kiss?
• Who was the first famous person you saw in person?
• Can you remember the smell of your mother's perfume?
• Whom did you like to walk home from school with?
• What was the best award you ever won?

If someone says, "Hawaii is like a slice of heaven," the minds of those listening quickly engage a variety of computations to make the statement understandable to them. Some might momentarily see a picture of their favorite place in Hawaii. Those who haven't been there might recall a postcard, film, or magazine picture.

Minds then must interpret the phrase, "slice of heaven." They might generate the smell of a piece of coconut-cream pie piled high with frothy meringue and recall a personal interpretation of what heaven is like. It doesn't matter how individual minds represent this phrase to those listening. The positive word picture it creates does have emotion attached to it. Charismatic leaders wouldn't just end here, however. Rather than using just a word or phrase that creates a positive emotion they would literally bombard the unconscious processes of listeners to create a storm of emotion in their minds.

Compare the following two examples. Notice the different ways your mind must work to create understanding of the answer.

Example #1

"Hey, Mike, how was the vacation?"

"Very nice, thanks, Tom. Hawaii is a beautiful place. Wendy and I came back really relaxed and happy. Mostly we just stayed on the beach and enjoyed each other's company."

Example #2

"Hey, Mike, how was the vacation?"

"Wow, was Hawaii a slice of heaven! Have you ever been on a perfect vacation? From the first morning we woke up there, all the stress from the past year just melted off. Can you imagine what it was like to wake up every day to the sound of crashing ocean surf and the smell of tropical trade winds? Wendy and I spent hours basking on the sun-bathed beach, rubbing each other with sun tan oil, and carrying on like two high schoolers. I'm a new man!"

Obviously, the second example creates a far more vivid picture in the mind of the listener. Tom's mind raced to find vivid experiences in his own past that were similar so he could uniquely interpret this response for himself. Each recalled experience probably included a vague emotional response. Some things Tom's mind might instantaneously have done:

1. Defined the phrase "slice of heaven."

2. Searched through memories to find *his* most perfect vacation.

3. Developed the sensation of stress "melting off his body."

4. Heard crashing surf and recalled the smell of a tropical breeze.

5. Felt the sun's rays on his body and the smoothness of oil on his skin.

6. Remembered a time when he had carefree fun in high school.

This occurs at blinding speed and outside conscious awareness, but it still creates an emotional impact on Tom. Most likely, Tom walked away with a pretty good feeling about this brief encounter. In the first example, the same basic information was exchanged, but it was done using logical, unmoving communication. Tom simply received surface information, cold facts. His mind was not activated to search for emotionally charged memories that would influence his mood, making him share the experience.

In situations when at least some excitement is expected from the person answering such a question, Tom might actually have walked away feeling confused or uneasy due to the lack of emotion in Mike's response. Tom might well ask himself, "He didn't sound very enthused about a week's vacation in Hawaii. What's wrong with that guy?"

ACTIVATING THE MIND

Using the language of emotional management activates the minds of those following your leadership as if they were super computers. The minds actually move into an altered state as they rush through endless files of memories searching for meaning to what is being said.

A growing body of evidence shows that the brain works faster and expends greater amounts of energy when exposed to this level of communication. It's as though hundreds of United Nations interpreters are all speaking at the same time in hundreds of different languages, working together to compose something making perfect sense.

The ideodynamic response works the opposite way as well. Think of a time you were around someone who was depressed, someone seeing only the bleakness of life. What happened to your state of mind after being with that person for a while? Most likely you too began feeling depressed, despite the fact there was nothing wrong in your life. This also happens because of the ideodynamic response.

Imagine that you overhear two people talking in a restaurant. You first notice them because of their contrasting physiologies. The woman is sitting straight but relaxed. The pleasant look on her face invites a smile in return. She speaks fairly quickly with a light, cheery tone. In contrast, the man's shoulders are slumped, his brow furrowed and his facial muscles slack. He speaks slowly, in a funereal tone. Their conversation goes something like this.

> SHE: I'm so glad you were able to join me for dinner. I really love this place, don't you?
>
> HE: Yeah, it's really nice. I wish I could afford to eat here more often.
>
> SHE: Well, I'm sure once you find a new job, you'll be eating in even better places than this.
>
> HE: I don't think I'm ever going to land another permanent job. I'll probably end up doing these hit-and-miss temporary jobs forever. There doesn't seem to be much point in even looking any more.
>
> SHE: Maybe you should think about starting your own business. Remember that I decided to become a consultant only after I lost my job. I figured I could make more money and never have to deal with another boss like Larry.
>
> HE: Start a business in this economy? I'd go broke. I'm really surprised you've managed to hang on as long as you have. Things must be really tough.
>
> SHE: Well, it has been a struggle, especially with my car loan and house payment ...
>
> HE: Boy, I don't know how you stand it. I'd be terrified of losing a client or not get-

ting new contracts. At least I don't have to worry about losing a house the way you do. I've given up on ever owning a house. I'll be happy to keep a roof over my head and not end up living in my car.

For the sake of your mental health, you stop listening at this point. The woman at the imaginary next table wouldn't be as fortunate. By the time they leave, her face would be tense and she'd probably look weary. No wonder. Consider the emotional assault she would have just been under.

In order for her mind to make sense of what the man was saying, she would have to think about or relive similar situations. The words and phrases the man used would force her to consider depressing thoughts and memories. Over what she had thought would be a pleasant dinner, she would find her mind filled with memories of an impossible boss and the inability to keep her job.

Then she would have to create pictures of the precarious economic times, the difficulty of meeting her financial obligations, and the uncertainty of her cash flow. To top it off, there would be the vivid image of losing the roof over her head and living in her car. Thinking about these events, either consciously or unconsciously, would produce the negative or depressing emotions attached to them.

Pretending we possess a magic wand, let's replay this conversation, hearing how it might sound if the man had a different outlook.

SHE: I'm so glad you were able to join me for dinner. I really love this place, don't you?

HE: Yes, it's one of my favorites. I miss coming here so often since I've been laid off.

SHE: Well, I'm sure once you find a new job, you'll be eating in even better places than this.

HE: I'm looking forward to that. Although, there is something to be said for knowing you're clever enough to get through rough times. I'm really learning a lot. Working for this temporary agency while I job hunt has given me some great ideas for jobs I never would have thought about before. I've expanded my job search and am seriously considering a career change.

SHE: Since you're exploring new ideas, think about starting your own business. Remember that I decided to become a consultant only after I lost my job. I figured I could make more money and never have to deal with another boss like Larry.

HE: Hey, that's a thought. I'm open to all ideas right now. That's one of the advantages of losing a job—you open yourself up to all kinds of new things. I remember a time you wouldn't even discuss being self-employed. Yet now you're thriving on it. I know you've had some concerns about the economy, but you're handling it just fine. In fact, you're a happier, more confident person now than you ever were before.

SHE: You know, you're right. I am happy and confident. I feel free and very much alive. I like living by my own ability. I think I'm better at what I do than I ever was when I had a weekly paycheck coming in.

HE: I never thought about it that way. I can see why you're blossoming. I'm going to start thinking of some ways I can pick up independent contracts while working these temporary jobs. Maybe before I land some great new job, I may just decide to open an office and fly solo. Let's toast to new possibilities.

Now, which man would you invite to sit at your table?

In Short

1. The hallmark of Charismatic Communication is the ability to manage the emotions of others. By being able to inspire powerful feelings in others you can assist them in becoming their best.
2. Emotional management revolves around one central phenomenon: the ideodynamic response. This is the ability of ideas and thoughts to bring out emotions in us.
3. Charismatic leaders manage the emotions of others by focusing their thoughts on emotionally driven themes, thus automatically inspiring those feelings within those around them.
4. Even during everyday conversations, as our minds decode the words of others, a wide variety of subtle and not-so-subtle emotions are constantly fired off. Charismatic Communication is simply the form of communication that focuses the minds of others on specific emotionally laden topics, thus creating the emotional state of mind desired, from being inspirational and motivational to drawing concern in others.

8

THE SIX CENTRAL TECHNIQUES OF EMOTIONAL MANAGEMENT

Charismatic leaders put the ideodynamic response to work inspiring the best in people. These leaders affix the minds of their employees, clients, volunteers, and loved ones on events and ideas that move them toward their absolute best. The fuse of excellence is lit by strategically crafted words and representations.

You too can ignite the passion and excitement others need for being their best. You can do this within moments by using any of the proven techniques in this section. You can inspire others to dive right into the pool of outstanding achievement.

But first things first. Before you can elicit the feeling(s) needed to achieve your desired outcome, *you have to know what outcome you want*. You must firmly plop the horse down before the cart. Sound elementary? Well, think back to all those boring staff meetings and presentations you've sat through.

Few of those leaders knew just what they wanted you to feel (much less how they wanted you to act) when they finished. That's because too many people never consider exactly what they want others to do as a result of their leadership. And you pay the price. Actually, so does the leader. You have an uninspiring experience, and the leader is left with mediocre or poor results.

Have we made our point? Just in case anyone missed it: *Knowing clearly and precisely what you want people to do is the first step in emotional management.* It is the foundation upon which you build strategies and presentations that bring the results you desire, every time. Once you know the desired outcome, you decide on the state(s) your listeners need to be in so they will *want* to take that action. Then you structure the method(s) you'll use to inspire those emotions. It's like connecting the dots. Get the picture?

Let's pretend you have a report to deliver, a speech to make, a sales presentation to prepare, a meeting to lead. You've decided your end result. You want people to buy something, support something, vote for someone, learn or believe something. Okay, now list the emotions you want them to feel. Here are some of the most useful:

Motivation	Desire
Want	Need
Joy	Entertained
Confidence	Passion
Curiosity	Experimentation
Love	Compassion
Excellence	Sorrow
Security	Perseverance
Focus	Humor
Flexibility	Creativity
Interest	Strength
Belief	Doubt
Confusion	Clarity
Delight	Fascination

You now have the outcome targeted and the states identified. You know where you're going, the horse is hitched to the wagon, and the wagon is loaded. But how are you going to get there? Don't worry. There's a map. It's comprised of six highly effective techniques. You can use them to take you right where you want to go. They are:

- Impact words
- Elicitation questions
- Sensory stimulating language
- Universal experiences
- Word pictures
- Stories

Using these methods, you can access any desired emotion in those with whom you come in contact and arouse in them the desire to forge ahead in your direction. Map in hand, you are on your way to becoming charismatic!

IMPACT WORDS: TURNING THE MUNDANE INTO THE SPECTACULAR

One of the easiest ways to generate emotional responses within people is to constantly use words that generate emotional impact. "Impact words" are those with which we associate either positive or negative emotions. For instance, when you speak of your "home" you evoke a stronger feeling than you do by calling it your "house." The reaction you get from saying someone acted like a "German soldier" isn't anything like saying that same person acted like a "Nazi."

For our purposes, we can say there are two kinds of words, experiential words and process words. Process words are those words that usually link thought and phrases together like "and," "the," and even the word "process." They have little experiential meaning to us. When you think of words like comfort, picnic, massage, or baseball, there are experiences we can attach to them already residing in our minds.

It is much more difficult to define a "process," an "if," or an "on." These words have an important role in language *structure* yet have no impact on human *emotions*. Even more unfortunate, our universities, government, and business institutions teach us a bland mode of communication focusing on the processing of language. For example, at a local city council meeting a career bureaucrat made the following statement.

> The objective of procuring additional materials to oversee the attainment of recreational goals through the direct and peripheral involvement of activist residents is proceeding and should continue to proceed within the necessary political constraints and desires of the council.

What he was trying to say was:

> Thanks to the enthusiastic neighbors who so willingly shared their time and talents, we're on target with the installation of state-of-the-art baseball, basketball, and football fields in Ranch Park. Thanks to the cooperation and support of the full council, this project was done in record time. I hear kids are already signing up for teams. We're also installing a fifteen-piece jungle-gym play area. In just a few more weeks, you can visit the park and see families spending time together as they picnic, hike, play ball games, and let the little ones play freely in a safe area.

Which one would you rather listen to? Which one would make you proud of your fellow citizens and good about your local government?

There's another difference between experiential and process words. The brain takes far more time to process emotionally charged words. Most likely this is because these words can't just be handled in the language centers of the left brain. To make full meaning of these words, both sides of the brain must be activated.

When a researcher flashes a set of words on a screen at a speed too fast to be consciously read, subjects require different amounts of time to process different words to which they were exposed. It usually requires more time to identify emotionally charged words than those that are emotionally neutral. "In essence, the brain analyzes the words for their emotional significance as well as for semantic features and patterns, before they reach consciousness." (Restak, 1991)

You have a much stronger effect upon people when you select and use experiential words. Most powerful are impact words that are capable of eliciting desired emotional responses. *These words are like triggers instantly firing off emotions and feelings.* Although each may vary in intensity, layering one after another has a cumulative effect on anyone. Every charismatic leader and professional speech writer knows that *how* you say something greatly affects response to *what* you are saying.

> **Words are among the primary tools of the charismatic leader. As with any fine craft, highest and best results are achieved when the right tools are selected for the job.**

Impact words have been skillfully employed for centuries by the great speakers of the world. When Franklin Delano Roosevelt was inaugurated as president of the United States in 1933, the impact words used in his inauguration speech began the process of bringing a nation paralyzed by the Great Depression back to its feet. [Emphases are ours.]

> . . . More important, a host of unemployed citizens face the *grim* problem of *existence,* and an equally great number *toil* with little return. Only a *foolish optimist* can *deny* the *dark realities* of the moment.

Yet, our *distress* comes from no failure of substance. We are *stricken* by no *plague of locusts*. Compared with the *perils* which our forefathers *conquered* because they *believed and were not afraid*, we have still much to be thankful for. Nature still *offers* her *bounty* . . .

. . . Happiness lies not in the *mere* possession of money; it lies in the *joy* of *achievement*, in the *thrill* of *creative effort*. The *joy* and *moral stimulation of work* no longer to be forgotten in the *mad chase* of *evanescent profits* . . . (Ravitch, 1990)

Theodore Roosevelt gave one of his most popular speeches on April 10, 1899, in Chicago: "In Praise of the Strenuous Life."

We would have avoided all this *suffering* simply by *shrinking* from *strife*. And if we had thus avoided it we would have shown that we were *weaklings* and that we were **unfit** to stand among the *great nations* of the earth. Thank God for the *iron in the blood* of our fathers, the men who *upheld the wisdom* of Lincoln and *bore sword* or rifle in the armies of Grant.

Abraham Lincoln's second inaugural address on March 4, 1865, is considered by many to be Lincoln at his best: simple, honest, and eloquent.

On the occasion corresponding to this four years ago, all thoughts were *anxiously directed* to an *impending* civil war. *All dreaded it*, all sought to *avert* it. While the inaugural address was being delivered from this place, devoted altogether to *saving* the Union without war, *insurgent agents* were in the city seeking to *destroy* it without war—seeking to *dissolve* the Union and *divide* effects by negotiation.

In Dr. Martin Luther King, Jr.'s famous "I Have A Dream" speech, he said

The *whirlwinds of revolt* will continue to *shake the foundations* of our nation until the *bright day of justice* emerges.

That has a lot more power than if he had said: "Those not content with the current situation will continue to protest until they receive what is rightfully theirs."

Impact words such as "whirlwinds," "revolt," "shake," "bright," and "emerge" create a more emotionally powerful message. Similarly, when Jesse Jackson spoke of the negative effects of television on the nation's youth he didn't say: "Young people depend too much on television." Instead, he referred to today's youth as "mass-media addicts."

Two of the charismatic leader's best friends are the dictionary and the thesaurus. With these reference books you can enhance any interaction, speech, or presentation with more powerful impact words. Words that define emotions are especially good to enhance the effect of what you say. For any word defining an emotion there are dozens of substitutes that generate a stronger impact in people. It's always a good idea to look up the impact word in the dictionary to be sure it's the right shading you want. Also, always keep connotative meanings in mind when selecting a word.

PLEASURE	COURAGE	WONDER	FEAR
Enjoyment	Bravery	Marvel	Scared
Happiness	Fearlessness	Stunned	Petrified
Bliss	Valor	Staggered	Panic
Elation	Fortitude	Breathless	Dread
Contentment	Pluck	Mesmerized	Chilling
Rapture	Grit	Awe	Eerie
Delight	Guts	Astonishment	Terror
Fun	Unwincing	Amazement	Nightmare

CHEERFUL	HOPE	LOVE	EXCITEMENT
Blithesome	Aspiring	Affection	Arousal
Lighthearted	Conviction	Adoration	Stimulate
Gleeful	Desire	Devotion	Electrify
Chipper	Expectation	Cherish	Thrilling
Vitality	Confidence	Yearning	Infuse
Zestful	Optimist	Passion	Effervescent
Perky	Supportive	Infatuated	Delirium
Merry	Assured	Idolize	Furor

THE QUESTION THAT CREATES ACTION

The use of questions is the simplest and most direct elicitation method. The power of questions lies in the fact that our emotions follow our thoughts. Therefore, *changes in what we think about cannot help but create corresponding changes in emotional state.*

Ask someone to think about a time when they felt totally loved or were very proud. Their thoughts will shift to occasions that aroused these emotions in them. Because of the ideodynamic response, they then reexperience the same emotions. *By asking the right kinds of questions, you can direct the thoughts of others, causing them to naturally change to the emotional state of mind you want.* It's that easy to gently move people's thoughts from their own agenda to yours.

Questions are a natural part of our regular communications with ourself and others. We are constantly trying to understand our world and those with whom we interact. An important part of this process is the constant asking and answering of questions in our head. In fact, much of our thinking process is made up of internal questioning. Even when we remain consciously unaware of them, the nature of these questions has a marked impact on our emotional state at any given time. "If he can do it, why can't I?" "What does that mean?" "Can I do it?" "What if I fail?"

Each time we ask ourselves a question, our mind searches through our memories for an experience to use as an answer. The way we phrase a question causes our minds to focus upon different kinds of memories. If we ask ourself, "How come I always screw things up?" our mind will search through the memories of when we did indeed screw things up. But if we ask, "How will I get a project this complex done on time?" our mind will search for memories and experiences of when we were able to get a difficult job done on time. *How we ask questions of ourselves results in accessing either powerful or negative emotions.*

Recent research indicates that when questioned, the human brain continues an exhaustive search throughout its entire memory system on an unconscious level. The mind apparently scans 30 items per second even when the person is unaware that the search is continuing to take place. The results of such searches on an unconscious level are evident from many familiar experiences of everyday life. How often do we forget a name or an item only to have it pop up all by itself only a few moments later, after our conscious mind has gone onto something else? How often are we consciously satisfied with a solution only to have fresh doubts and perhaps a better answer come up autonomously a short while later? (Erickson, Rossi, and Rossi, 1976)

This information is significant to the charismatic leader. Since thoughts direct emotions, *you can bring about virtually any emotional state in others by asking the correct questions.* Everyone in your audience has memories. These memories are full of feelings and emotions. *You want to elicit memories that have attached to them feelings useful to your goals, your leadership.* Your job is to have the audience remember such memories and focus on them.

A salesman who wants to elicit a positive buying state in an audience might ask such questions as

Do you remember how we once thought that not only was a computer too expensive for business, but we'd never be able to learn to use one? And now that we've had one for awhile, don't you wonder how you ever ran your business without one?

Sometimes it's difficult to know which is the right decision to make. Think about a time you had an important decision to make and the one you made was exactly right for you. Can you remember the factors you considered when making that decision? What made you finally know you had done the right thing?

By asking such questions, you begin to access memories that will elicit the emotional states of mind accompanying decisions that turned out well. This helps calm the sometimes irrational fears people have of making decisions or making a change. People are then open to the presentation of your product and feel confidence in their ability to make the right decision.

EXERCISE

Think of five questions you could ask that would leave someone feeling great!

The elicitation of emotions through questions is effective. As a very direct method, however, it has weaknesses. For it to work, you must have developed *strong* entrainment with your listeners. Since people's conscious minds are alert and filtering like crazy, they are looking for the intent and deeper meaning of everything being said. Consistent use of overt questions can cause people to consciously analyze your deeper intent for asking. This can destroy the impact of the question itself. Given this limitation, before using this technique, it's important to be sure you have established strong entrainment.

> *Charismatic communicators are masters at skill-fully asking questions. They get others to auto-matically recall memories that have specific emotions attached to them. Almost instantly, a common emotional state begins surging through everyone listening.*

Be aware also that during any given encounter, meeting, or presentation you may need to elicit a number of different emotional states to reach your goal. Used alone, elicitation questions can lose their effectiveness after being used more than two or three times. Once again, your audience, employees, or clients may become alerted to your intent for asking these questions.

SENSORY-STIMULATING LANGUAGE: HOW TO ENERGIZE THE MIND

It is generally more effective to use subtle methods when eliciting emotions in people. Such a message moves unchallenged past the filtering processes of the conscious mind as it communicates at a deeper level. Such a powerful and subtle technique is the use of vivid descriptive words that literally stimulate the senses of your listeners. Sensory stimulating words are those that tend to activate one of our senses.

As a word is spoken, our minds activate as they attempt to translate the sound into a meaningful representation. Each sensory system can be activated by different types of words. For example, the word "twinkle" is associated with the visual sensory system. We don't hear or feel a "twinkle," but we can *see* something twinkle. In the same respect we *feel* a "twitch," and hear a "shrill." But we don't see either one. To be translated effectively, specific words must be processed by different functions of the brain.

When you use vivid sensory-oriented words in your descriptions, you stimulate and arouse a powerful mental response in others. Whenever you give an example or make a description, you have ample opportunity to use sensory-stimulating language. This language activates and stirs vivid representations in the mind of each individual.

Sensory-stimulating language helps the mind push away from the logical communication and processing of words. It activates the senses of listeners. For example, to say, "He had a bothersome voice" provides very little information at a deep neurological level. However, if you say "He had a shrill and abrasive voice," the minds of your listeners have something to do. They recall what "shrill" sounds like and what something "abrasive" feels like.

Of course, this usually happens beyond conscious awareness. It nonetheless has a striking effect on people. Sensory-stimulating language defines experiences in ways they can be understood. It also provides people the chance to "personally" understand what you're saying, as your words force their minds to search for experiential meaning.

EXERCISE

Next time you're reading a good novel or poem check and see how many times the author activates the senses in your mind on each page.

This traditional technique has been used by virtually every great charismatic leader. It is usually most effective to focus on visual, auditory, and kinesthetic (feelings) words. An example would be:

VISUAL	AUDITORY	KINESTHETIC
See	Hear	Feel
Reveal	Shrill	Grate
Clear	Quiet	Solid
Flash	Banging	Strangle
Twinkle	Resonate	Hard

On June 6, 1984, Ronald Reagan delivered a speech on the fortieth anniversary of the Normandy invasion. In this excerpt from that speech, his uses of sensory-stimulating language have been marked out:

We're here to mark that day in history when the Allied armies joined in battle to reclaim this continent to liberty. For four long years, much of Europe had been under a terrible shadow[V]. Free nations had fallen[K], Jews cried[A] out in the camps, millions cried[A] out for liberation. Europe was enslaved[V], and the world prayed for its rescue. Here in Normandy the rescue began. Here the Allies stood[K] and fought against tyranny in a giant undertaking unparalleled in human history.

We stand on a lonely, windswept[V] point on the northern shore of France. The air is soft[K], but forty years ago at this moment, the air was dense[K] with smoke and the cries[A] of men, and the air was filled with the crack[A] of rifle fire and the roar[A] of cannon. At dawn[V], on the morning of the 6th of June, 1944, 225 Rangers jumped . . . (Reagan, 1989)

In this example, President Reagan uses a number of sensory-stimulating language techniques to move his audience. In the second sentence, the word "shadow" describes the tyranny of the war that had been waging. Shadows are often something we see rather than hear or feel, in this case giving us a representation of oppression. This automatically attaches a level of discomfort toward the war.

He then takes us on an experiential trip where we hear the desperate cries of people stand firm against evil and see the windswept beach where war once raged. In actuality, very little tangible information was delivered in this speech. Yet it's still wonderfully moving. Reagan guided everyone through a vivid internal experience. The experience had a different yet similar meaning for each individual because of the strong internal representations tied to the words.

The Bible, one of the most enduring and influential documents on earth, uses sensory-stimulating language to ensure full understanding by every reader. In hundreds of passages it deals with the visual, auditory, and kinesthetic processing of information. For example, in the fourth chapter of Proverbs, verses 20 to 26, it says

> Be attentive to my words; incline your ear to my sayings[A]. Let them not escape from your sight[V]; keep them within your heart[K]. For they are life to him who finds them and healing to all his flesh[K]. Keep your heart with all vigilance; for from it flow the springs of life[K]. Put away from you crooked speech, and put devious talk far from you[A]. Let your eyes look directly forward and your gaze be straight before you[V]. Take heed to the path of your feet, then all your ways will be sure [K].

It would have been easier to write this passage without the inclusion of the main sensory-stimulating categories. However, the writers of the Old and New Testaments were somehow inspired to communicate in this manner. It is a style with which anyone is able to form strong internal understanding of the information—even centuries later.

Spoken or written, sensory-stimulating language is powerful. It causes both sides of the brain to function together. Words structured in this fashion carry similar emotional impact for everyone listening. The appropriate feelings are automatically elicited as a by-product of the vivid thoughts people create in their minds as they listen.

That's why it isn't necessary for you to have a sympathetic audience. In order to understand your words, even people who don't agree with what you are saying have to make the appropriate representations internally. They can't help it. It's the way their brains work. As they listen, they will experience emotion even if they disagree with the words of the message. This happens because these language patterns, by their nature, stir specific feelings.

When employing this technique, it is usually best to use sensory-stimulating language in one category at a time. You can start, for example, with visual, then move to auditory, then kinesthetic. It doesn't matter in which order you use them. But to elicit the most potent thoughts possible, it is usually most effective to separate the descriptions. If at first this seems redundant, persevere. As you begin to see the results, satisfaction will more than compensate for your efforts. The more you employ your creative powers, the greater the impact you will have on your audience.

UNIVERSAL EXPERIENCES: RE-CREATING THE POWER OF LIFE

Universal experiences are events so common in life they happen to most of us at one time or another. The states of mind generated by these experiences are also similar. Universal experiences generate similar feelings and are shared by many people. Therefore, recalling them results in evoking a fairly common state or feeling throughout a group.

Only a small percentage of people knows what it's like to huddle sick and cold on a dark street with no one to turn to for help. Likewise, only another small percentage knows what it feels like to live in a penthouse with servants and a chauffeured limousine at their disposal. In other words, these are not universal experiences.

In this country, however, the majority of people have a driver's license. All people can recall when they first began driving on their own. Those feelings will be fairly similar among all (excitement, independence, accomplishment). Most people have fallen head-over-heels in love at least once. Love evokes certain feelings in human beings, feelings to which everyone can reconnect readily.

Using universal experience to elicit the same specific emotion in a group is powerful. You pull the group together, bringing it to a common emotional state. Actually, the group does it for you. All you have to do is talk about these universal experiences. People will instantly access their individual memories of the event. They cannot help but feel the emotions associated with it. That's powerful communication!

President John F. Kennedy, lobbying for America's push into space, drew upon a number of then recent events in a speech at Rice University. Each of these technical events awed the American public as they witnessed man moving toward the unthinkable dream: landing on the moon.

> We have felt the ground shake and the air shattered by the testing of a Saturn C-1 booster rocket many times as powerful as the Atlas which launched John Glenn, generating power equivalent to ten thousand automobiles with their accelerators on the floor. We have seen the site where five F-1 rocket engines, each one as powerful as all eight engines of the Saturn combined, will be clustered together to make the advanced Saturn missile, assembled in a new building to be built at Cape Canaveral as tall as a forty-eight-story structure, as wide as a city block, and as long as two lengths of this field. (Sorensen, 1988)

Dave Thomas, founder of the Wendy's hamburger chain, has recently used a variation of this technique in a series of popular TV commercials. In his book, *Dave's Way*, he talks about his success with this style of advertising.

One of our ads has me eating at a gourmet restaurant where I'm shocked at the small portion size. Everyone has had that experience. You go into a fancy restaurant and the waiter makes fun of your French. The garnish is bigger than the entree, and when they give you the bill, you wonder if you get to keep the silverware. We've all had experiences like that. (Thomas, 1991)

When identifying universal experiences to elicit the emotions you desire, you should remember two important points. First, there are literally thousands of universal experiences that people in your group share. However, many of these experieces—such as combing their hair or washing dishes—have little or no emotion attached. They don't really serve your purpose. What you need are universal experiences that elicit strong emotional states every time they are thought about.

EXAMPLES OF *ELICITATION TECHNIQUES*

(Remember, entrainment must be present to achieve full impact)

CURIOSITY

QUESTIONS:	Can you remember a time when you were totally curious? When you had that feeling of complete and unabated curiosity? When you just had to know?
UNIVERSAL EXPERIENCE:	Can you remember years ago when you were a kid, and it was a few weeks before Christmas? You knew your parents had gone shopping for your Christmas present. Can you remember what it was like to *wonder* what they had bought you, feeling as if you couldn't stand one more minute of not knowing just what it was?

Can you recall what that felt like? What you said to yourself?

EXCITEMENT

QUESTIONS: When was the last time you were really excited? I mean a time when you just wanted to jump around and scream. You know, that time when your adrenaline was flowing, when it felt as if your heart was about to jump out of your chest. When was that time?

UNIVERSAL EXPERIENCE: Remember the first time you rode on a roller coaster? The long, slow ride to the top, then the rush of adrenaline as you went plummeting down! The clatter of the cars flying over the track as your vision blurred with the force of the wind in your face. Maybe you put your arms over your head as your ears filled with the clatter of the cars on the track and the screams of the other riders.

PRIDE

QUESTIONS: When was the last time you felt really proud of yourself? Maybe you did something that at first seemed impossible? Or you achieved what everyone else said was impossible? Remember when you knew you had done the right thing? Can you recall just how that felt?

UNIVERSAL EXPERIENCE: Remember watching the Olympic torch being carried from one end of this country to the other? Remember how it felt watching Americans from all backgrounds, races, and colors, even those in wheelchairs and on crutches, handing the torch of liberty, freedom, and the will of the human spirit from one to another? Can you still see those final few steps as the torch was brought to the Olympic stadium to mark the beginning of the games?

EXERCISE

Try this. Think up a few emotions you may want to elicit in others, such as desire, anxiousness, or just general good feelings (see the following). Then write down a variety of questions and universal experiences that would focus people's minds on such emotions. Remember, these techniques work splendidly when entrainment is present because people then naturally follow those things asked.

DESIRE

QUESTIONS: What is your most compulsive habit?—Can you remember the feeling as it's coming on? If you could go out and buy one thing right now regardless of price what would it be? Can you remember those times when you just had to go out and buy something?

ANXIOUSNESS

QUESTIONS: Do you feel you have enough time in your day? Have you ever sat behind someone at a stoplight who wouldn't go? Or what about being late for an appointment and being stuck behind a slow car? It's like waiting for a really important phone call that never comes.

GOOD FEELINGS

QUESTIONS: What would constitute a perfect day for you? What do you like best about your life? What does it take for you to feel totally successful? Who is the person who had the most significant influence on your life? If you were given a chance to relive any part of your life, which part would it be?

WORD PICTURES AND STORIES: RADIATING ENERGY WITH YOUR WORDS

What makes perfect and clear sense to us doesn't necessarily make any sense to others. That's because all of us have composed our own individual "rules" of logic. These rules guide us through life, telling us what we should or shouldn't do, buy, or believe. They let us know when it's appropriate to feel a certain way. They allow us to like or dislike something or someone (and tell us why).

It's easy to see why leaders attempting to use logical reasoning when convincing others to take action have a difficult (if not impossible) job. Visualize each person's system of logic as a laboratory mouse maze. Logical reasoning requires you try getting through that labyrinth of "logic" using the system that is uniquely yours. You're using the map of your maze to guide you through 10, 50, or 200 other mazes that are different not only from yours but different also from each other. It's the stuff of which nightmares are made.

There you stand before a group comprised of individuals with their diverse systems of logic chugging away. You want to say something that will change their behavior or cause them to leap into action. Now you understand why it's an uphill battle to convince them logically. So what are you supposed to do? You do what great charismatic communicators have been doing for centuries. *You spend no more than 10 percent of your speaking time on logical issues.* Instead, you use your time to employ powerful communication tools that actually get results.

Among the most powerful of these tools are word pictures and stories. These tools have been around about as long as the human race. In fact, *since man first developed language, word pictures or stories have been used to shape people's actions, behavior, beliefs, and values.* Crafting and weaving colorful tales that ring true for everyone listening has created transformations nothing short of magical.

If you pay attention, you'll see *the hallmark of almost every charismatic leader is the ability to tell captivating and inspiring stories.* You've seen it happen. In the mouth of a skilled communicator, the story takes on alchemical properties. Even the driest topic is transformed into a vision of depth and color that seduces people, moving them where the leader desires. Appropriately used, word pictures and stories take all the previously reviewed elicitation techniques and wrap them in an interesting story for the pleasure of those listening. At the same time, they induce strong internal changes within people.

When people hear word pictures and stories, their minds become fully stimulated. Their minds create vivid internal pictures, sounds, and feelings in order to understand what is being said. People don't just listen. They become part of the story, participants. The story keeps the conscious mind interested and entertained while indirectly communicating your point to the unconscious mind.

The great thing about stories is that they by-pass the filtering systems of the conscious minds. You avoid the busybody interference of the conscious mind. *Stories allow you to impact the unconscious level.* There, specific states of mind are elicited and people make new internal associations. Aren't stories handy things? Isn't it time you began using them more?

Word Pictures

Word pictures are usually simple one or two sentences that capture the attention of those listening while engaging thoughts and feelings. Use word pictures and you transform mere words into something valuable.

During his presidency, Ronald Reagan created the word picture of the Soviet Union as the Evil Empire. Instead of talking long and dryly about the differences between the Soviet Union and the United States, he created this simple, two-word analogy: Evil Empire.

It isn't surprising that a nation immersed in the trends created by the powerful and popular film *Star Wars* grasped this word picture to its heart. Almost overnight, it became a powerful generalization in the minds of Americans across the nation. Many of us could no longer hear the words Soviet Union without seeing George Lucas's imposing Death Star. We felt the hate spewed forth by The Force's dark side. We heard the whooshing sound of Darth Vadar's mechanical breathing as he strode toward inevitable confrontation with the forces of good. Using two words, Reagan succeeded in creating an internal association that whipped past all logic, creating a powerful and vivid internal experience.

Dictators ride to and fro upon tigers which they dare not dismount. And the tigers are getting hungry.

Winston Churchill

Let us not seek to satisfy our thirst for freedom by drinking from the cup of bitterness and hatred.

Martin Luther King, Jr.

America's not a blanket woven from one thread, one color, one cloth.

Jesse Jackson

But now the winds of change appear to be blowing more strongly than ever, in the world of communism as well as our own.

John F. Kennedy

Word pictures bring thoughts to life, creating a more vivid and powerful image. You've been using them ever since you were a child to relate other classes of experience to the issue at hand. For instance, when jilted by a lover, we say we have a *broken heart*. Something simple is like a *walk in the park* or a *piece of cake*. When delighted we're *tickled pink* and when life is going well it's a *bowl of cherries*. When applying pressure to get something done or make a group accountable, we *hold their feet to the fire*.

By simply increasing the use and sophistication of word pictures, you have more influence over how people think and feel about you and your leadership. Word pictures can best be used to create an emotional response in your listeners by activating thought processes, senses, and emotions. For example: instead of saying:

Unless we receive these additional funding requests we won't be able to continue the project at the state-of-the-art level it was developed.

You could say:

Not providing additional funding for this project would be like developing and building a Porsche and then hitching up a horse to pull it because you don't want to spend money on fuel. This project has the power and sophistication to put us far ahead of our competitors with their horses and buggies. So let's fuel it up and get going.

Instead of saying:

I need each of you to get out there and drum up some business. Come on gang, let's get excited!

You might say:

I'm as excited about going after those new sales as I ever was at the beginning of a marathon. We've been preparing for months. We've stretched out. We've warmed up. We've studied the course. We're ready! Now it's time to lace up our shoes and hit the pavement. No one has a better team, a sharper team, a better prepared team. So let's focus all that training, all that energy, all that drive on the goal ahead: to reach those new customers before the competition ever leaves the starting line!

Word pictures can create a new frame or context for what you say, radically changing the way people view you and their participation. For example:

Let me show you the plans for our new marketing strategy. With strict adherence it should be quite profitable for each of us.

or . . .

We've got a great new marketing game plan for you. We're giving you some powerful plays designed to make sure you score big over and over. I think once you look at it you'll see how, with our coaching and your expert team, we'll all end up champions.

***

Jerry, I think we need to talk about your performance over the past few months. Quite frankly, it just hasn't been up to our standards. Can you tell me what the problem is?

or . . .

Jerry, over the past few months you're like a thorough-bred race horse who has injured his leg. You're just not turning in your usual championship performance. What can we do to get you back in the winner's circle?

Word pictures and stories create new understand-ings and powerful emotions without the use of logical argument.

Word pictures can also be successfully used in larger contexts rather than in short sentences or phrases. Abraham Lincoln's 1860 speech at New Haven, Connecticut, is a won-derful example.

. . . If I saw a venomous snake crawling in the road, any man would say I might seize the nearest stick and kill it; but if I found that snake in bed with my children, that would be another question. [Laughter.] I might hurt the children more than the snake, and it might bite them. [Applause.] Much more, if I found it in bed with my neighbor's children, and I had bound myself by a sol-emn compact not to meddle with his children under any circumstances, it would become me to let that particular mode of getting rid of the gentleman alone. [Great laughter.] But if there was a bed newly made up, to which the children were to be taken, and it was pro-posed to take a batch of young snakes and put them there with them, I take it no man would say there was any question how I ought to decide! [Prolonged ap-plause and cheers]

That is just the case! The new Territories are the newly made bed to which our children are to go, and it lies with the nation to say whether they shall have snakes mixed up with them or not. It does not seem as if there could be much hesitation what our policy should be! [Applause] (Fehrenbacher, 1992)

EXERCISE

Think about the most complex aspect of your job. Find four different ways to describe it using word pictures from each category below.

- **A sporting event**
- **Cooking**
- **A relationship**
- **An animal**

Stories

The stories used to elicit emotions are even more powerful than word pictures. They captivate the mind for longer periods and delve deeper into the emotions of the listener. What's more, stories can include all the previous elicitation techniques to create even greater impact. Once again, the goal is to imprint a vivid picture on the minds of your listeners, drawing out the needed emotions.

Have you ever seen the Walt Disney movie *Bambi*? Can you recall how you felt when Bambi's mother was shot by the hunter? When *Bambi* was first shown in movie theaters, the only sound heard was the crying of children and, in many cases, the adults who had accompanied them. Well, the impact of *Bambi* was felt far beyond the theater.

The year before the animated film was released, deer hunting in the United States was a $9.5 million business. But, when one particularly touching scene was shown—that of a yearling who sees his mother gunned down by a hunter—there was a dramatic change in many men's attitudes. The following season, deer hunt-ers spent only $4.1 million on tags, permits, and hunting trips. (Smalley and Trent, 1988)

Stories can radically change the behavior of people by touching their emotions, the origin of their actions. Start by identifying or relating to incidents in your own or other's lives that created certain emotions. You can then begin to develop your own repertoire of elicitation stories for a variety of purposes.

Stories in the form of metaphors have long been used to elicit emotion and action. In their book *Metaphors We Live By* professors George Lakoff and Mark Johnson wrote that human beings define reality in terms of metaphors. They then proceed to act on the basis of them. The metaphor even serves as a guide for future action, which then reinforces the power of the metaphor.

"In this sense metaphors can be self-fulfilling prophecies," say Lakoff and Johnson. According to them, "We draw inferences, set goals, make commitments, and execute plans, all on the basis of how we in part structure our experience, consciously and unconsciously, by means of metaphor."

They offer the example of President Jimmy Carter's declaring "the moral equivalent of war" in response to the nation's energy crisis. This led to the imaging of an "enemy" and "threat to national security." There was a setting of "targets," marshaling of "forces" and imposing of "sanctions."

Lakoff says, "The metaphor was not merely a way of viewing reality; it constituted a license for policy change and political and economic action. The very acceptance of the metaphor provided grounds for certain inferences: there was an external, foreign, hostile enemy . . . ; energy needed to be given top priorities; the populace would have to make sacrifices; if we didn't meet the threat, we would not survive."

Additionally, stories can be used to teach others how to behave and react in the future. A counseling friend received a phone call from a distraught mother of a high school student. The mother had been upset by her son's consistently low grades and disciplinary problems. She was now embroiled in another battle—his insistence on playing guitar in a local rock band. The counselor asked a series of questions about the quality of the friends he would be playing with and the level of dedication he was putting into his music.

The mother was surprised to be told, "I think it's a great idea. Let him play!" The councelor knew this was a young man with low self-esteem. She also knew people could succeed in virtually any endeavor if they have the drive and belief that they can. But beliefs come from verifying experiences in our past. If we have succeeded various times in our past, we believe we can succeed in other challenges in our future.

This young man had never felt good about his academic abilities or many other things in his life. When people fail time and again, they come to believe they will continue to do so. So the first step was to build up a series of experiences and memories that created powerful examples of the young man's ability to succeed. The counselor had the wisdom to know that the young man badly needed to have experiences of successes in his mind. What the endeavor was didn't matter. Because, once we know we can do something well, know we can achieve, we develop the courage to use those same skills in other areas of our lives.

The people who follow your leadership are no different. They need the experiences of successes to function at their best. As a leader you have two options. Create an environment where people continuously succeed at everything (realistically impossible) or use the age-old technique of great leaders: stories. Remember that stories, when delivered well, are accepted into the minds of your listeners as though they were real experiences. By constantly feeding their minds with success stories (or any other needed kinds) you can give them years of positive experiences in a matter of minutes. You can give them the tools to succeed in whatever endeavor is required.

EXERCISE

Create a notebook full of great inspiring stories.

Where do you find such stories you ask? Everywhere! They abound in our everyday life. On television, radio, in the newspaper, in your own life. We are too accustomed to saying to ourselves, "Isn't that a neat story?" and then forgetting about it. Don't! Cut them out, write them down, and get them in the notebook. Keep them sorted by emotional impact. Remember to keep searching for these mentally nourishing tidbits.

When giving a speech or presentation how many stories or word pictures should you use? How long should you talk? A good rule of thumb is the following:

USE OF WORD PICTURES AND STORIES
(in minutes)

	STORIES AND WORD PICTURES		LOGICAL INFORMATION
Entertainment and broad leadership speeches	3–4 minutes	per	1 minute
Standard business presentations	1–2 minutes	per	1 minute

STACKING: ENSURING SPECTACULAR RESULTS

It doesn't matter if the setting is a conference room, classroom, church, television studio, or living room. When we communicate with groups, our primary job is to elicit the states needed to achieve our outcome. Eliciting states is an important part of any communication. It's imperative to know that you have fully elicited the desired state(s) in everyone. "Stacking," or combining the six elicitation techniques in conjunction with one another ensures that you reach everyone in the group.

The truth is, even using a universal experience to elicit a specific state won't guarantee you've reached everyone. It doesn't matter how much you plan and how carefully you construct elicitation techniques. It is virtually impossible to generate a strong state in everyone using just one technique. After all, there *are* people who have never driven a car, fallen in love, or ridden a roller coaster.

> *By constantly using and stacking these techniques, you will find those you lead becoming more and more inspired to dedicated, enthusiastic action.*

That's why you use several elicitation techniques to spice up your presentation. It's like creating a wonderfully rich sauce. You use a little of this, a pinch of that. You ask a few direct elicitation questions, then use a metaphor centering around a universal experience. Then finish off with another question. However you mix and match, always cluster at least three elicitation techniques together. That ensures good audience penetration without spending an inordinate amount of time.

LEARNING FROM SOME OF THE BEST

Theory, books, and education are an excellent way to introduce new information into our lives. Yet, quite often such information doesn't translate into real-world applications. It just doesn't seem to work.

The research necessary to complete this project, however, started from the opposite direction. It started with the individuals doing it, not in a laboratory setting. We started with charisma and then backtracked to break down and define the components. We tested the process each step of the way. Rather than coming up with theories and attempting to prove them, the Charisma Factor was the product of close observation in the world backed with the supporting scientific theory. For that reason, it now is easy to identify the how's and why's of charisma and how it can work for you.

Reagan vs. Carter—a Charismatic Comparison

On November 4, 1991, Presidents Bush, Reagan, Carter, Ford, and Nixon came together at one time in Simi Valley, California, to dedicate the new Ronald Reagan Library. This event provided a wonderful opportunity to compare the communicative leadership abilities of each president. Reagan, the Great Communicator, literally flooded the minds of his listeners with elicitation techniques, taking each one on an emotional roller coaster. Carter, who was branded by Reagan in the 1980 campaign as a "caustic pessimist," demonstrated his style of speech making: purely logical. You be the judge as to who had the ability to touch the hearts and minds of their audience.

Impact Words*—Asterisk
Elicitation questions—Bold
<u>Universal experiences—Underlined</u>
Sensory-stimulating language—^{VAK}
Word pictures and stories - Italic

Ronald Reagan
(Spoken in a perfect entraining rhythm)

They will be able to trace the historic process *by which mankind has stepped back from the narrow window ledge of* *mutually assured destruction.* <u>They will observe an American President and a Soviet leader sitting in a boat house on the shore of Lake Geneva striving to banish the *nuclear nightmare* from the dreams of all our children. They will see^V tears of pride from the boys of Pointe du Hoc. They will hear^A the trusting^{K*} engines of Challenger lifting off on a heart-breaking* final mission. They will be introduced to a warm^K and selfless* First Lady who reached out to a generation of young Americans threatened* by the scourge* of drugs and who put a comforting^K arm around an older generation through the Foster Grandparents Program. They'll catch the sinister* crackle^A of a would-be assassin's* weapon, one that forever changed the lives of Jim and Sarah Brady</u> while reconfirming my belief that whatever time remained to me was to be spent in service to the American people and in accord with the Lord's wishes.

No doubt many visitors will stand in the replica of my oval office. Perhaps they will sense a little of the loneliness* that comes with decision making on a global scale*, or the *stabbing^{K*} pain inflicted* by a terrorist bomb* half a world away, or the dreaded* sound^A of the telephone in the middle of the night with news of hostile* actions. They will also feel^K some of the immense* pride that comes to any president in that office as he comes into daily contact with the American heroes* whose faith in themselves, their mission, and their mandate is a never ending source of emotional renewal*.

Jimmy Carter
(Spoken without a definitive rhythm)

We still struggle* together, Democrats and Republicans alike, on basic issues that affect our country, the insurance of military strength. All of us who have been in office know that to plan, design, test, and produce a weapons system, as those used recently in the Gulf, it takes several presidential administrations to bring those dreams into reality, that our fighting men and women have a chance to prevail*.

Let me point out that we still have some unanswered questions: How to provide good health care for all our people, homes for those who don't have a place to dwell, better education for our children. These are the kind of things that make a common tie among all us presidents who have served.

I would say parenthetically that one of the things that brings former presidents closest together is the extremely onerous and burdensome* task of begging* for enough money to build a presidential library from private sources; not from the government, and then turn it over to the federal government in perpetuity as a repository for the records of our great nation. (Source: Federal News Service)

John F. Kennedy

My friends: I close on a note of hope. *We are not lulled** *by the momentary calm^K of the sea or the somewhat clearer^V skies about. We know the turbulence*^{K} that lies below^V, and the storms* that are beyond the horizon this year. But now the winds of change appear to be blowing^K more strongly than ever, in the world of communism as well as our own. For 175 years we have sailed with those winds at our back, and with the tides of human freedom in our favor. We steer our ship with hope, as Thomas Jefferson said, "leaving Fear astern."*

Today we still welcome those winds of change—and we have every reason to believe that our tide is running strong[K]. With thanks to Almighty God for seeing us through a perilous* passage, we ask His help anew in guiding the "good ship Union." (Sorensen, 1988)

Patricia Schroeder

This is a defense budget with no priorities* and no discipline*. *It's a Twinkie defense. It's like a child loose in a pastry shop. Even if one swallows hook, line, and Trident* the Reagan-Weinberger *sermon** on the national-security need for increased defense spending to meet the Soviet threat*, the Administration still ought to be able to reform*, terminate* or cut* those Department of Defense activities least useful to defending America in order to provide more money for those programs most useful to defending America. (Shafritz, 1990)

In Short

1. **There are six main linguistic techniques in emotional management.**

    Impact words

    Elicitation questions

    Sensory-stimulating language

    Universal experiences

    Word pictures

    Stories

2. **Impact words and sensory-stimulating language are better suited for generating a general heightened emotional state of mind. Elicitation questions, universal**

experiences, word pictures, and stories work best when inspiring specific emotions.

3. These techniques can be used alone or in conjunction with one another. However, there should be at least three attempts at eliciting each particular emotion to ensure coverage of everyone.

9

ADVANCED EMOTIONAL MANAGEMENT TECHNIQUES

Charismatic leaders are by no means restricted to mere verbal techniques in order to inspire a wide range of emotions. In fact, they often rely on a variety of other verbal and extraverbal methods that work with stunning speed and consistency. Let's take these pages to focus on another series of techniques you can use every day.

EVERYDAY CHARISMA

Charismatic communication isn't something you pull out to use in speeches and presentations and then tuck back in a tissue-lined box for the next special occasion. In fact, for charismatic leaders there is no such thing as just another everyday interaction. Rather, they recognize that *there is something special about every exchange with every person.*

An interaction can be personal, managerial, supervisory, or leadership related. No matter, for it to work we have to care. And what we care about must be more than getting what we want, short-term productivity or popularity, or today's receipts. Charismatic leaders know something that others tend to forget. *Superior productivity, quality, and results (and ultimately profits) all come through one source: people.* And, when it's all said and done, nothing is more important for guiding people than the dictates of their hearts. For that reason, charismatic leaders constantly focus on the emotional state of mind, the mood of people around them.

What really matters in achieving the best possible results is having people whose hearts are in what they are doing. When charismatic leaders see someone whose heart is somewhere else, they know they must reach this person at the emotional level. To do this, they must communicate emotionally through charismatic communication.

To be effective, the emotions you elicit in others don't have to be attached to the job at hand. For example, if an employee seemed depressed and weren't doing a good job, you wouldn't need to discuss job performance or the source of depression. *Your job is simply to assist others in feeling better, more resourceful, inspired, and motivated so they are able to do their best.* Actually, it's easier and more effective to change their mood by dealing with something different than to focus on the current problem.

> *The job of the charismatic leader is not to be a cheerleader, but to constantly refocus the minds of those around him or her so their natural energy, excitement, and enthusiasm come out.*

Think about a time you received a nice compliment or something wonderful happened in your life. Didn't it change your mood for the day, week, or even month? Didn't you feel almost like a different person? The truth is *when we feel differently we act differently.* We work harder, act more kindly toward others, willingly take that extra step.

Emotions control the level of effort human beings put forth and the quality of work they perform. *Even the simplest word or action can tip the scale, improving or worsening someone's outlook and ability.* You can bring people up to their greatest possibilities or down to their lowest levels. You have a choice.

Knowing the danger contained in the venom of negativity, charismatic leaders quickly interrupt negative thinking in their employees, clients, donors, or constituents. They then focus thoughts on more positive and empowering ideas. By doing so, they consistently increase the productivity and satisfaction levels of people. They create a positive environment and become an important and valued person in others' lives. *The one who can consistently bring others up to their emotional and professional peaks is rare.* As with anything uncommon, a high value is placed on the charismatic leader.

INSTANT CHARISMA: WHEN YOU BECOME THE ESSENCE OF INSPIRATION

In the previous chapter, we reviewed a number of linguistic techniques for managing the emotions of others. There are, however, a variety of other methods that can be just as effective. There are a number of ways to quickly create more positive emotions in others. When you couple them with other emotional management techniques you'll be amazed at how fast they work.

Are you a watcher of television talk shows? If so, you probably can't count the number of times you've watched comedians talk about fans who burst out laughing the instant they encounter a favorite comedian on the street. The comedian doesn't have to be doing or saying anything funny, or even making an overture to a joke. What is it that makes people laugh simply at the sight of the comedian?

Or think about seeing a picture or hearing a recording of someone who touched you deeply. When you look at the picture or listen to the recording you begin to feel those same feelings again. How is it that no matter the context, some people move others powerfully just by being seen or heard?

When something affects you emotionally in any way, your mind is aroused to a greater extent than when no prominent emotions are present. *The greater the emotional impact, the stronger the activation of the brain.* The high emotional content of the memory causes it to be etched deeper and more permanently into the brain. *This means the use of emotionally based communication causes you to have a far stronger and more lasting effect upon others.*

When our eyes look at someone we've had dealings with before, our mind goes through a variety of speedy memory searches looking for previous encounters with that person. It's how we identify who people are and establish our relationship with them.

As we know, when the brain does such searches it also brings up the emotions attached to those memories. That's why we can walk up to a person and immediately be filled with warm, happy feelings. And why we can walk up to someone else and have feelings of depression or anger creep up. It all depends on the many emotionally laden memories connected to that person.

As we go through each day, there are countless changes and additions to the neurological networks making up our memories. *Our experiences alter and change millions of neurons, millions of brain cells.* Some events are new or unique. They create whole new neuro-networks. Other events, interactions, and tasks are routine or similar. They only strengthen existing neuro-networks.

One cell from one network influences the reactions of surrounding cells. It becomes easier and easier for these common responses to occur time and again. This is how habits are created. For example, though there may be several good routes you could drive to work, you probably have one you drive daily without thinking about it. Your thought processes about driving to work have, over time, been sufficiently strengthened to become a habit and are therefore automatic. In the same respect, picking up your coffee mug each morning and filling it may be far more a habit built from repetition than from thirst or a liking for the taste of coffee. It's just another example of how *consistent occurrence, experience, or behavior is so thoroughly etched into your mind you can function automatically.*

When people watch and listen to charismatic leaders, they are touched by the message. A powerful memory is formed. A cluster, a network of neurons, becomes dedicated to memories of that leader. In that network reside the words, voice, sights, and feelings surrounding him or her. With each additional contact and renewed uplifting of emotions, that network is expanded and strengthened. It's as though charismatic leaders make a wonderful holograph in the minds of all those with whom they come in contact.

Over time and with multiple contacts (especially those that are emotionally laden) it becomes almost habit, a conditioned reflex, to instantly feel good, proud, powerful around that person. The leader's persona, voice, person fire off the wonderful feelings embedded in the neuro-networks. They have become the essence of charisma.

Imagine helping people feel better, work stronger, be more themselves. Aren't these gifts beyond price? They can't help but make people feel good. This translates into feeling good about yourself, because you were the one who made the effort to free those emotions. In time, your presence begins to fire off the same sensations. You don't even have to do anything at that moment to warrant it.

By consistently having a charismatic effect on others, you come to embody those traits in their minds. Just seeing you, hearing your voice, the shake of your hand or the smell of your cologne can trigger off those same feelings. This is when you become a stunningly powerful leader.

EXERCISE

Take a moment and think about the kinds of emotions you are etching into the minds of those you lead. Are they the kinds of emotions you want them to instantly feel in your presence? Are they conducive to your power as a leader?

If not, begin making every interaction with them filled with those specific emotions. Create for them at "habitat" of feeling confident, powerful, inspired, or excited just by your presence. You'll be amazed at the long-term results for your organization.

ENTRAINING EMOTIONS

In order to explain the tools of charismatic communication, we had to break them out separately. In reality, they all work together. *Your personal congruence coupled with entrainment is the catalyst for inspiring others.* When you master the skills of personal congruence and entrainment, you can guide the emotions of others almost instantly.

When human beings listen to words, the language centers in their left brains are stimulated to decode information. Simultaneously, their eyes and ears pick up extraverbal information, vocal quality, facial expression, and so forth. This grouping of information is processed in the right brain, the side where emotions reside. Both sides of the brain are activated in the decoding process, always checking with the other part to see if the messages mesh, if they're congruent. Here's where our congruence is made or broken.

That's why entrainment is so critical to the process. *When there is synchrony in the pulsating brain waves of the people involved, a bond is created.* Conversations and speeches become far more than a sharing of words. They are the sharing of experiences. You deeply connect with others. You also communicate in a very human, natural, and powerful manner. Add entrainment and you are not only *communicating* with your emotions, you're *sharing* your emotions with others.

EXERCISE

People are often concerned about knowing if they have truly entrained with someone or not. Here's another way to test for entrainment and at the same time complete the emotional management phase of charismatic communication.

Next time you're having a casual conversation with someone begin syncing with them, maybe using a rhythmic voice and matching their posture. After a few minutes of conversation, when you're feeling comfortable, shift the subject to something you're excited about, maybe a new house you're buying or a promotion you just got. If they, too, become excited (you'll know by their own congruence), then you know you've successfully entrained and that you're now fully into the realm of charismatic communication.

Remember, it really can be as simple as that. Once you've introduced positive emotions into the interaction you're having a charismatic impact. Keep building on that initial success and notice how they begin responding to you.

In fact, one way to tell if entrainment has taken place is to see if your emotions affect those with whom you converse. *If people are entrained, they will share much of the emotional content as well as the words of a message.* Should one person become excited about something, the other will get excited as well. Or, if one becomes concerned, the other will follow suit, regardless of the topic.

With entrainment established, bringing up positive and powerful emotions in those around you can be easy to do. You may first speak in an easy, flowing, and distinctive rhythm that slowly draws people toward you. Once they are there, you can talk about something that motivates you, excites you, makes you proud. You will then be able to infuse those emotions in others as well.

We all know people who have an enthusiastic outlook on life. They uplift those around them just by being there. These people have a natural ability to entrain easily with others. Then, when they are expressive about *any* subject, they naturally guide the feelings and emotions of others up to them. These are the people who have natural charisma every day.

THE SCHWARZKOPF SYNDROME

In January 1991 Americans found themselves transfixed before their televisions watching Cable News Network. Newscasters in a Baghdad hotel room relayed the frightening images of our military forces committed to war. During the following weeks we remained spellbound as bombing raids continued. We wondered what would happen. Would Saddam Hussein use chemical warfare? Would our soldiers be able to cross his impenetrable line? How many of our young men and women would be killed? And would our country once again suffer a rout in front of the world?

Emotions soared. We were restless, troubled, fearful. We no longer live in a world where wars can be contained in isolated geographic areas. There are missiles, terrorism, biological and nuclear warfare. There were no safe boundaries. What we needed most was to know there was someone in charge. Was there a *real* leader or simply another bureaucrat or politician calling the shots? Were we walking into another Viet Nam?

Then General Norman Schwarzkopf strode into view on television screens across the world. His large stature and burly build fit many people's imagined picture of the classic military leader. He was wonderfully congruent. He told us things the way they were. He pulled no punches, provided no double talk.

Somehow, *he instantly created in the minds of millions the perception that he was the one in charge.* Everything about him said we could put our faith in his leadership. There was something in his relaxed confidence that for the first time in a long time let us breathe a sigh of relief. America had found the kind of leader for which it had been searching.

A brilliantly executed battle plan led to a swift victory. The world was elated. We had been spared the most horrible potentials of war. And America had emerged strong, powerful, and proud once again. As we felt these emotions surge through us day after day, we began to associate them with one man: General Schwarzkopf.

He was the one in charge. He was the one we trusted. He provided us with the vital information we so desperately needed. In a short time, the man himself became the symbol of pride and confidence for many Americans. Simply seeing him on television let us relive those feelings.

Does this mean Schwarzkopf is a charismatic leader? Not necessarily. He *is* a powerful and congruent leader, a brilliant military mind. Yet he never displayed all the classic traits of the charismatic leader. Instead, he was a leader thrust into an emotionally charged environment. *By taking the positive leadership role, he became the focal point of that event.* When all was said and done, we tended to associate the success of the event with the man. Seeing him and hearing his voice caused us to reexperience all the powerful emotions of that time. At a deep level, we even attributed its success to him.

Many leaders have achieved much of their power and acclaim through this phenomenon. For example, Lee Iacocca had always been a strong leader, but when he pulled Chrysler from the brink of extinction he became a hero. When asked to list charismatic leaders many people will include movie stars. Are they all charismatic? Most often they are not. But the movies people see them in send intense emotions surging through their bodies time and time again. Being human, people normally associate those feelings with the star rather than with the film itself. So when some people think about the star they feel much the same way they did while watching the movie. The *effect* is charismatic.

EXERCISE

Imagine that your company was in dire financial straights due to a dramatic drop in market demand for key products. How could you best make use of the Schwarzkopf Syndrome to lead your company back into health?

Many leaders have done well by themselves and their careers when they stood up and took a positive leadership role in an emotionally driven situation. By steering their organizations and followers clear of harm's way and into brighter waters, they benefited from the relief, excitement, and joy of the situation.

MANAGE THE BODY: MANAGE THE EMOTIONS

The primary focus of this book has been on using thoughts to generate positive emotional reverberations. There is another factor that also elicits and inspires more resourceful emotions in others. In fact, it is the fastest way to change emotional states of mind. Most people will tell you they feel better when they take a brisk walk or work out. This is true because both activities change the speed, rhythm, and tempo of the human machine.

Emotions are much like small chemical eruptions in the brain. When changes in the body's position and speed of movement are made, different emotionally stimulating chemicals are introduced. *The more powerfully you use your body, the more resourceful and positive chemicals surge through it.* Consider how much of performance is based on emotional state of mind. What does a culture like Japan's— legendary for its high levels of individual performance on a daily basis—do about workers' state of mind? For consistent results, Japanese leaders must daily elicit the most positive emotions in employees. They must ensure that workers leave behind personal concerns, anxieties, and fears so they may focus on performance.

What do Japanese leaders do regularly that American supervisors do not? Simple. Many Japanese companies start their day with one ritual: exercise. No matter what mood workers arrive in, strenuous exercise creates the physical movements of power, confidence, and focus. *Exercise is, in effect, massive physiological change. It introduces natural mood altering chemicals into the body.*

Exercise isn't the only way to do this. *Motion of any kind effects change.* Even the mere physical act of smiling has been proven to uplift the emotional state of a person. As we know, there is a natural push toward congruence, a drive for mind and body to function in unison. Think about a political convention. Did you ever see one where all participants were sitting down? Not likely. Emotion and the body go together. *We cannot be in the physiology of one state and feel the feelings that accompany another.* For people to be in powerful, resourceful emotional states they must move and flex their bodies.

What is the link between movement and emotion, between mental and physical functioning? As human beings, we all share pretty much the same neurological system. Our "hardwiring"—brain, nerve endings, senses, and electro-chemical processes—are all but identical. These systems facilitate all our thinking mechanisms and control the physical movements of our bodies.

Remember a time you were with someone who was depressed? Think about his physiology. Were his shoulders slumped? Did he tend to look down? Was his face rather slack? His breathing shallow? Were all his movements slower, heavier? These are just some of the normal physiological traits of depression. Now think about a time you felt elated. Maybe you won an award, received special recognition, or accomplished something at which you had worked very hard. As you think about that time, remember your physiology: the way you stood, your posture, gestures, facial expression, breathing rate. Was it a strong physiology, one that makes you feel great just to remember?

Like depression and elation, *each human emotional state has a certain and specific physiology hardwired into it*. When we focus internally on something powerful, our mood, our emotions change. There is an infusion of chemicals in our brain. These chemicals send specific electrical impulses throughout our nervous system. As these unique signals are sent out, among other things they instruct our bodies how to move and position themselves.

We can identify emotional changes by observing the unconsciously controlled physiological changes they create. These include posture, skin tone, pupil dilation, muscle tension (especially in the facial region), breathing rate, and vocal quality. A number of these changes occur when we are in any given emotional state. We each have our own unique combination used to express a particular emotion. The end product, however, will still be fairly similar to other people's for the same emotion. It's as if we have the same basic model car or home but customize it to make it uniquely ours.

What does all this have to do with charismatic leadership? Does it mean that you must conduct an aerobics class prior to giving a speech or starting the workday? No. But it does provide you with a variety of additional options for shaking people out of a negative mood. What do you do when children are inside moping around? You tell them to go out and get some fresh air, ride their bike, go see a friend— do something, anything.

Funny thing is, when the children vigorously change their physical position, posture, and so forth, they can get into a much better mood. The same thing is true of employees or co-workers. If someone is sitting behind a desk feeling depressed, ask her to walk downstairs with you as you go to a meeting. Get her to help move something or file some papers. If you need to arouse an audience, use alignment techniques that move them around. This not only will expand their mood, it will help assert your leadership.

During a union meeting when the membership was split pretty evenly on an emotional issue, an astute leader brought the group back into good cheer. It's often difficult to run a meeting where half the attendees are passionately opposed to the desires of the others. In such situations it's imperative that issues be talked out. The leader cannot allow negative emotions to spill out and engulf everyone.

During this particular meeting, both sides wanted to be cooperative. But after a while they began to lose patience and became irritable. This led to feelings of anger directed at the "others." The meeting leader sensed he was about to lose control. What did he do? He simply interrupted the rhythm of the group. Everyone was invited to get up and take a break by stretching at their seats. Since people were uncomfortable with the negative emotions, they welcomed an opportunity to turn away from the meeting for awhile.

Everyone stood, stretched, began to chat, and some even laughed. Five minutes later the meeting resumed. Negativity had dissipated. Members were ready to once again talk about solutions. Simple? Yes. But it worked to maintain an effective meeting. This leader shook his members out of their negative emotions merely by changing their physical positions for a few minutes.

EXERCISE

Next time you're at a gymnasium compare the faces of people when they arrive in contrast to when they leave. Is there a big difference in their emotional state of mind?

As we know, it's imperative for charismatic leaders to first match individual people where they are (especially emotionally). It is then possible to move them gradually to a more appropriate state of mind. For example, if someone's depressed the last thing he or she wants is someone else to come bounding up with reassurances that everything is going to be just fine. In this case, you would first match much of the person's behavior. You could talk at the same tone and tempo, sit in relatively the same way, and use the same kinds of gestures. Then you would move to using syncing techniques. Once the two of you were entrained, you could gradually begin using emotional management techniques to bring the person back up.

Depending on your discussion, such a gradual change in emotional state might go like this:

- Depression to . . .
- Unhappy to . . .
- Feeling low to . . .
- Interest to . . .
- Intrigue to . . .
- Enthusiasm to . . .
- Motivation

Once you're proficient in the skills taught here, helping a fellow employee or friend move from depression to motivation could take as little as ten to fifteen minutes, depending on the situation. By using physiological change you can substantially speed up the process. Just by getting a depressed person out and on a walk while you talk with him or her may eliminate any negative emotions in only a few minutes.

- Depression to . . .

Introduce vigorous physiological change

- Interest to . . .
- Intrigue to . . .
- Enthusiasm to . . .
- Motivation

BABY HARP SEALS: THE METAPHOR THAT CHANGED A NATION

All the leadership traits and strategies from every book and seminar ever written or presented are useless if your leadership isn't *accepted* by those you would lead. Consider the ecological movements of the 1970s. The groups' members had a clear direction. They knew what they wanted and were congruent about it. Yet most made little headway in those early years.

Think about news clippings from that time. Do you remember seeing fragile rubber rafts bobbing in choppy waters? Their crews struggled to remain between whalers' harpoons and animals the whalers were intent upon killing. Or recall the sight of a fishing vessel sinking after being rammed by a boat filled with protesters intent upon stopping the killing of dolphins in tuna nets.

Obviously, these people were passionate. But they didn't have a connection with mainstream America, those they needed most to influence. *They lacked acceptance.* In their zeal, these groups had neglected to first position themselves in a leadership role for all of America. They committed a cardinal sin of would-be leaders. Both as groups and individually *they set themselves apart from rather than aligning with those they wanted to lead.*

Still, concern for the preservation of the ecological system has become a major issue in American thought and politics. These same groups came to have a major impact on the consciousness of our nation and the world. How? First, they dropped their militant stance. Through a number of steps they then raised the general public's awareness level. They showed how what was happening environmentally was in direct opposition to basic American values.

A turning point in the movement was the campaign to stop the slaughter of baby harp seals for their fur. The groups portrayed the events in relation to some of the strongest values of mainstream America. *They created a perfect metaphor.* The drama played out on television screens, in magazines and newspapers across the nation and the world.

We saw helpless baby seals looking up innocently at rough, hulking men who then clubbed and skinned them. Some mother seals were shot as they rushed to protect their infants. Others sat on blood-soaked snow holding mournful vigil over the skinned bodies of their babies.

Americans who believe in the sanctity of motherhood, protection of the young and helpless, and who root for the underdog were horrified. *Through this unconscious assault upon some of its deepest held values, America's consciousness became forever altered.* When environmental groups moved into the political arena, they had what they most needed— the solid backing of mainstream America.

EXERCISE

What are the values your company's actions portray to your clients? Do they coincide with the clients' values?

If not, what new courses of action could you implement to remedy that problem?

By creatively matching their cause to the deeply held beliefs and values of the nation, ecological groups were able to gain credibility and prominence. By identifying the beliefs and values of your audience and then crafting your message to fit with those, you will instantly induce the powerful emotions attached to them. The charismatic effect will be fast and automatic.

GETTING CREATIVE WITH YOUR ENVIRONMENT

There are many numbers of ways to elicit different emotional states of mind. You can often do it without saying a word. It can be done with the creative use of sight, sound, feeling, taste, and smell.

There are many things in our environment that automatically cause us to feel certain ways—a song, the smell of a specific perfume, a movie, a roast beef dinner. These are universal experiences of sorts. For example, the movie *Rocky* pumped up many viewers. A large part of that experience was the theme music, "Gonna Fly Now." Many of us have heard motivational speakers play that theme just before they come on stage. They obviously intend to elicit the same strong feelings in their audience these people had when they saw the movie.

Another elicitation technique used by many is the use of selected movie clips shown when the group needs to be in a specific emotional state. There are hundreds of popular movies from which they choose. Any popular movie is seen by a wide range of Americans who felt joyful, sad, compassionate, hopeful, excited, powerful, or motivated during the movie. These turn into universal experiences of sorts and are often used at rallies, conventions, and political events as a way of augmenting the enthusiasm already present.

What may be the most pervasive method for arousing specific emotions through an entire group is to actually create an environment that automatically elicits emotion. As an example, during a political clash between city hall and a political action group, the city officials became pictured in the press as a noncaring group with no heart. As is often true, the facts of the issue mattered little. Popular opinion was slipping rapidly away. The opinions of the press, the public, and the political action group needed to be changed and changed quickly! A public meeting was scheduled to give those concerned an opportunity to meet with elected officials.

Here's where an entirely different perception could be created in the minds of everyone involved. We started by moving the gathering from the city's formal meeting room to a restaurant's banquet area. We borrowed antique chairs and tables, and covered them with tablecloths. There was a fire in the fireplace. Soft music played in the background. We asked members of an uninvolved community group to help by coming in to bake pies and brew coffee right there. Elected officials brought their families. Everyone was dressed casually. There wasn't a basic gray business suit in sight.

When our guests arrived, the first effect was confusion. Remember, the vision they had was of this government entity as cold, uncaring, untouchable. The environment was unexpected, counter to all their perceptions. They were immediately struck with an overwhelming experience. The whole room interrupted their thinking.

Once inside, there was no head table to focus their political attacks at, no line dividing "them" and "us." The elected officials were dispersed around the room with their families. The participant's senses were assaulted with warm, comfortable associations from the fire, decor, smells of coffee and pie, and the music.

Everyone had the opportunity to eat and relax. Then, one by one, the elected officials walked around the room and talked about their point of view in a conversational manner. The results were spectacular. That night elected officials and the political action group came up with a solution that is still in effect today. Additionally, the press gave the meeting rave reviews. Citizens who attended expressed renewed confidence in their local government.

As is often the case, the issue was not differences in opinions. It was about inaccuracies in perceptions. Since the issue wasn't based on logic, it couldn't be solved with logic. It could be solved only where it lived: at an emotional level. We helped to create the feelings in the group that allowed for constructive discourse to occur. We gave everybody an opportunity to win. If we create total environments focused at eliciting certain states of mind, we give an entire group the opportunity to accomplish much more.

Disneyland uses these techniques in the waiting areas of their new rides. Visitors entering the usually enclosed waiting areas are surrounded by a sight and sound extravaganza designed to create a state of anticipation. The designers use what used to be waiting time to enhance the visitors' overall experience. They create an environment that places people in a specific state. Waiting in lines has been turned into a positive part of the Disney experience.

Whether you have 1 or 10,000 listeners, inspiration is the most effective method of motivating them to do the things you want done. With the variety of elicitation techniques available, charismatic communicators are limited only by imagination and flexibility. As long as elicitation techniques are stacked to ensure strong penetration, you will achieve consistently remarkable results.

EXERCISE

Look around your place of work and see what you can do that would automatically infuse new emotions in your clients and employees.

ERADICATING NEGATIVITY IN SECONDS

Even with the most powerful of charismatic leaders there are times when customers become angry, clients feel doubtful, supporters get disappointed, and employees stagnate. Negative emotions, regardless of how hard we try, creep into our sphere of influence. They attack in countless ways, such as through nasty rumors, fear of the economy, office politics, an argument with a spouse, or even too little sleep. People, your people, are under attack every day and once in a while they succumb, no longer having the capability to provide their best efforts. Whether they are afflicted with the funk of depression, the grip of fear, or the pierce of anger, it often becomes the job of the charismatic leader to assist them in getting back on their feet and to provide the emotional boost necessary for them to once again want to strive for their greatest efforts.

Yet, when dealing with someone caught in a negative frame of mind, it becomes difficult and extremely time consuming to infuse positive feelings even when using emotional management techniques. You need a way to quickly "break" people out of the grip of negativity; to buoy them up from their emotional depths. In essence you need the tool that quickly pulls people back, giving you the opportunity to reinvigorate them. You need to be able to make their negative thoughts disappear, to make them go away, quickly! A manager need not be a therapist. There are times when people do need to vent, but productivity is usually hampered not by severe emotional trauma but by the effects of everyday stress. Fortunately, there is a much better way to help people get their spark back. It is fast, effective, and, best of all, it respects people's privacy and dignity.

From previous chapters we know that emotions are directed by thoughts. Through the ideodynamic response, thoughts create the feelings that surge through our bodies. They can give us the energy to carry on, or they can create the walls that block even the smallest progress. It is precisely for this reason that charismatic leaders strive to alter the thoughts of others through emotional management techniques.

There are several names for this technique, but the one we like the best comes from a certain charismatic police chief. This chief had the uncanny ability to walk into some of the most hostile political situations and in a short time defuse their feelings and gain their support. When he was asked about his unique ability he said, "I just don't let people hang on to bad thoughts. I keep *diffusing* their negative thinking till they can't remember why they were mad. After that it's easy to begin talking."

When he talked about "diffusing" negative thinking what he was really doing was saying or acting out anything he could think of that was so compelling, so extraordinary, so different, so shocking, or so confusing that he completely captured the attention of others. In essence he was a master at subtly, yet radically, changing what people were thinking about. By doing so he was able to alter their feelings so they would forget about being upset or depressed. Because they were no longer focusing on negative thoughts they were no longer caught in negative feelings.

Diffusion works because any time people interact there are a number of behavioral patterns that we expect from the other. For instance, in Western cultures, when two people meet there is the expectation that they will shake hands, exchange certain pleasantries, look each other in the eye while speaking, and exhibit countless other minute behaviors that are ingrained through our cultural training. When someone strays from these cultural expectations, however, our thoughts are uncontrollably drawn away from the topic of conversation to that unexpected behavior. If you have ever been in face-to-face conversation with someone raised in an Arab culture you know that their comfort zone is only inches away. Culturally, they were taught to maintain what Westerners consider an inappropriate distance during casual conversation. The unsuspecting Westerner, despite his best efforts, will find it extremely difficult to maintain a coherent train of thought because of the discomfort it creates.

Diffusion works on the same principal yet is usually more subtle in application. Have you ever been sitting through a long, monotonous lecture when someone entering the back of the room slammed the door? What happened to everyone's attention? Or have you ever had someone you've never laid eyes on briskly walk up and vigorously shake your hand as though you're old friends? What happens to your concentration then?

Our thoughts and emotions are often diffused and changed in response to our external world. Things people say; the way they say them; how or where we are touched; sounds, situations, and experiences all can have an effect on us. The trick is to understand this basic principle and use it to release others from the bondage of negativity. If, for example, a worker is upset by the cancellation of a contract, her performance could fall sharply. Simply by dwelling on the situation over and over her mind will automatically fall into an upset emotional state that will result in poor performance. By defusing her focus on the troubling matter, a positive state and therefore quality productivity can return.

The charismatic leader, recognizing a negative pattern, can quickly assist the employee in feeling better about herself and jumping back into the game. The process of diffusing negative emotions is comprised of *three quick steps*. The first, as with all other aspects of charismatic communication, is to develop entrainment. Although not absolutely necessary, it does make the process go much more smoothly.

The second step is the actual diffusion of the negative thoughts. Later in this section we will review a variety of techniques that will get you started. But the most important point to remember about diffusion is that you can do virtually anything that will redirect their thoughts as long as it doesn't break the entrainment between the two of you. Should you see a fellow employee unsettled over a poor evaluation, you wouldn't want to walk over and slap him hard on the back in an effort to redirect his thoughts. Certainly he may momentarily forget about the evaluation, but he would be less than happy with you over the sting in his back. Sublety and sensitivity are the answer.

Remember, your job is to captivate, not alienate.

The third step is to quickly redirect the thinking process to a new focus. One student told us a story of how she hated going out to dinner with her parents because they constantly argued with each other. Prior to the training she felt she had no tools available to take control of the situation. Once she became adept with diffusion, however, she did not experience that loss of control again. As she related it, "We had just been seated at our table when Mom and Dad started at each other again. As I browsed through the expensive menu, their tone kept getting harsher and their voices louder. Sensing a momentary lull in the conflict, I slapped down my menu and stated matter-of-factly that I was going to have the peanut butter and jelly sandwich. Stunned, my parents stared blankly at me as I began excitedly talking about the amount of protein in peanuts and the health benefits derived from them. Then I turned to my father and asked how our family doctor was doing. As we talked about our old doctor friend it was obvious that Mom and Dad had completely forgotten about their differences and we had, for the first time in ages, a nice meal!"

What this student did was a perfect execution of diffusion and redirection. By asking for peanut butter and jelly at an expensive restaurant and then going right on to talk about related health aspects she completely threw off her parents. They were captivated by the unusualness of the topic and situation. She then redirected their thinking by asking about their old friend the doctor and engaged them in the new topic. She jolted their thoughts away from their disagreements and redirected them on to a new and more positive conversation—a simple, fast, and graceful way to get control of a bad situation.

Diffusion can be anything that is so compelling, so extraordinary, so different, so shocking, or so confusing that it instantly captivates the mind of everyone around you.

Diffusion works in much the same way strong changes in physiology do. They speed up the process when helping someone move from a negative emotional state of mind to a powerful one. Notice in the following how it shortens the motivation chain.

Normal Emotional Progression Using Only Emotional Management Techniques	Normal Emotional Progression Including Diffusion Techniques
Depression to...	Depression to...
Unhappy to...	Diffusion to...
Feeling low to...	Intrigue to...
Interest to...	Enthusiasm to...
Intrigue to...	Motivation
Enthusiasm to...	
Motivation	

Although diffusion can be anything that captivates the mind without breaking entrainment, there are some broad categories that can help you develop a number of strategies yourself. The categories are *Compelling, Contrast,* and *Confusion.*

Compelling Diffusion

Compelling diffusion is something you do or in which you engage others that is so compelling that their minds become completely engrossed in the subject. When an infant cries adults tend to put on a variety of funny faces and make playful squeaky noises in an effort to divert the child's attention. It is a natural method we use to become so compelling that we diffuse the thought of whatever is making the baby upset so that the child becomes engaged in the distraction.

Adults occasionally interact with each other in the same way. Have you ever watched people who were so into what they were talking about that you became almost mesmerized? Their animated gestures, voices, and facial expressions became so compelling that others were absorbed by their presence. Communicating in this fashion is a simple but effective form of compelling diffusion. In fact, maintaining a strong level of personal congruence tends to act as a compelling diffusion all by itself. As humans we are naturally drawn to those whose movements, behavior, and actions are powerfully focused in one direction.

Another way to employ compelling diffusion to eliminate negative emotions is to provide people with intriguing projects when they're in need of a boost. A manager we have worked with who oversees a department of computer engineers now keeps a number of interesting and extremely involving projects at the ready. Whenever a unit's productivity begins to falter due to a reduction in enthusiasm the manager assigns one of these projects with which he knows the unit will become absorbed. The total focus these interesting projects require act as a natural stimulant for the group.

EXERCISE

Think about those things in your everyday life that are naturally compelling. How can you use them to captivate the attention of others and boost sagging morale?

Examples of compelling diffusion:
        Highly animated communication
        Total congruence
        Fascinating stories
        Intriguing projects

Contrast Diffusion

Contrast diffusion is that which violates the normal expectations of everyone. During a summer camp for junior high schoolers the head counselor was trying to make a series of announcements in the mess hall. Despite his best efforts to get their attention, the campers continued to carry on as if he weren't there. Finally, out of desperation, he lunged onto a large hanging lamp out in front of the stage and, while swinging, calmly made his announcements to a perfectly quiet audience.

Although we seldom find ourselves in situations where such extremes are called for, this example points out an interesting phenomenon. When you give speeches or presentations and feel that you are losing some control over the attention of the group, simply move to a location where they would not expect you to be. By moving to an unexpected location you will catch their attention and diffuse any stray thoughts. Feel free to jump off the stage and continue as you stand in the middle of the audience. Sitting for a while on the edge of the stage or in a seat may cause the same effect. Just find any location in the room where you would not be expected and go there.

Also think about the effect of noticeable changes in the tone, tempo, or volume of your voice. Or, if you stand up and walk around the room for no apparent reason, what happens? Talk-show host Phil Donahue regularly diffuses the attention of his audience when the focus shifts too far from him or he when begins to lose control of the room. He will suddenly ask an outrageous question or make an extreme statement. At this point all eyes and attention move instantly to him.

Another Donahue technique is to use a strange tone of voice and draw out a word while using it. "Weeeeeeell," he will say, sometimes adding an expansive physical movement such as flinging his arms up in the air and walking briskly out into the audience. Donahue also uses large and unique physical gestures like bending over at the waist and curling into himself. All these are examples of diffusion. They take the audience's attention off what it's on and moves it back to where Donahue wants it: on him.

Examples of contrast diffusion:
Speaking from unusual locations
Unusual changes in vocal tone, tempo, or volume
Facial expressions that contrast with the situation
Unique body movements

Confusion Diffusion

Confusion is one of the most powerful methods of diffusing negative emotions. Because people are always seeking the meaning of their experiences, they will go to great lengths to mentally search for understanding of any situation. *You can quickly diffuse the negativity of anyone or any group by strategically confusing and then redirecting their thoughts in new directions.*

Confusion diffusion can best be accomplished by saying things that, although delivered with total sincerity, really make no sense. In this way people most often begin an exhaustive search in their minds in an attempt to discern what has been said so as not to look foolish by not understanding "simple English." The moment that mental search starts, the negative state of mind begins to disappear (or diffuse) because of people's inability to think about two things at once.

Imagine an irate customer returning a defective product to the store manager.

CUSTOMER: I have just had to drive forty-five minutes out of my way because *your* lamp that I just purchased at *your* premium prices doesn't work! I want to know how you are going to compensate me for the lamp, my time, and gas!

MANAGER: Oh, no. I am so sorry for the inconvenience. Every once in awhile, regardless of how hard we try to ensure that tomorrow's successes are yesterday's finest products, we have something like this happen. I will be more than happy to personally make sure that you have at home exactly what you thought you had in the store before you got here.

CUSTOMER: What do you mean?

MANAGER: I want to make sure this doesn't happen again as you get home. (Beginning to provide direction). So would it be okay with you if I have our best installation man come to your house first thing in the morning with a brand new lamp and professionally install it at no cost? That way I will know for sure that you got exactly what you wanted in the first place.

CUSTOMER: (Understanding the manager's offer) Oh, ah, well, yes. That would be very fine . . . Thank you so much.

This type of diffusion can work comfortably in virtually any situation. Just make sure that when people begin to get a confused, inquisitive look on their face you begin to provide them with a direction. College professors are often great at the confusion technique without meaning to be. On the first day of school any freshman class is a sea of blank stares. Already disoriented, students listen to the professor use one large word after another in an unfamiliar context. There is now confusion. Students cannot grasp the meaning of what is being said. The problem is, professors seldom take advantage of this situation by giving students a firm and positive direction. When a state of confusion has been created but no direction is given people become alienated from their leaders, as they tend to feel inferior instead of bonded with them.

This is too bad, because *when people are in a state of confusion, they accept virtually any new topic that can introduce an entirely new set of feelings and emotions.* For example, a colleague once found herself in the midst of a hostile union issue representing management's concerns to an unfriendly group. In such volatile situations, if there are to be productive results it is essential to remove the hostility from what preceded to allow people to begin discussing the issues constructively.

Before long, a particularly hostile person jumped up shouting. There are several options for dealing with people like this. Our colleague chose a diffusion using confusion. This would allow for returning the group to a more productive emotional state. As the hostile person finished his tirade, she walked a few steps closer to him and in a completely congruent manner said:

> I understand your point, and I wonder what's really important here that you just have not been thinking of right now that will change that situation? And while you're collecting those things, I was also wondering just how you were able to ensure that the information that you heard was correct prior to your first exposure to it? Because, as we all learn about the complexities of this issue, we know that we cannot not learn, so it seems really important for each of us to know what we've learned to know what is appropriate.

Remember that her tone and manner were normal, no different from everything she'd said previously. The room was silent. The entire group looked blank. They were confused because the tone and manner said, "This is normal speech," yet their minds could not make sense of the words. In the midst of this confusion, she said in a slightly lower tone of voice:

So it would be okay to sit down and begin listing those successes the company has had this year. And that way we can begin to determine how to continue so we will all benefit from our efforts.

Since this was the first thing she had said that did make sense, the man complied with the request.

EXERCISE

Practice each category of diffusion in an off-the-cuff fashion 10 to 15 times a day. When you can successfully move through all 3 steps in a few seconds you will know that you have mastered the technique.

Examples of confusion diffusion:
> Any series of statements that almost make sense but don't
>
> The use of extravagant vocabulary that others don't understand

Diffusion is limited only by your imagination. It can be used time and time again to help manage the emotions of any number of people. The more outrageous and off the wall it is the more potent the impact. This ensures everyone's interest is captured and they are looking toward you for meaning. *The only boundaries for diffusion are good taste and the maintainance of entrainment with the group.*

In Short

1. **By consistently impacting people at an emotional level they become conditioned to feeling certain ways simply by your presence. The more methodical you are at inspiring those around you the faster they will develop**

this conditioned reflex that makes your charismatic presence instantaneous.

2. The combination of congruence and entrainment is all that is needed to infuse emotions in others. By creating a strong entrainment bond and then beginning to speak congruently about a subject that is emotionally important to you, those entrained will also begin to feel the same way.

3. Any time there is a situation where emotions are running high and you provide quality, ethical leadership to see the group through, you too will be considered charismatic. Those being led will attach the powerful feelings of the situation to you.

4. Never forget that there is an unbreakable link between our physiology and our emotional state of mind. If you want to quickly break people out of a negative state or augment an elicitation sequence, get them to move their bodies. The more vigorously they move the better they will feel.

5. By simply crafting your message around the deeply held values of your audience, you can create powerful responses instantaneously.

6. Remember that there are a multitude of things in our environment that evoke emotional responses. By creatively using them with a specific purpose in mind, the environment will do the work for you.

7. To dramatically speed up the process of emotional management, you can use diffusion to eliminate negative emotions in others. Working on the same principles as standard emotional management techniques, diffusion quickly pulls people out of their slump.

THE CHARISMA FACTOR

THE CHARISMATIC PERSONA
OPTIMISTIC LANGUAGE
PASSIONATE COMMITMENT
EMOTIONAL EXPRESSIVENESS
PERSONAL CONGRUENCE

CREATING THE BOND ⟶ **CHARISMA**
PHYSICAL SYNCHRONY
VOCAL SYNCHRONY
MATCHING SKILLS
GROUP ALIGNMENT
ENTRAINMENT

THE MANAGEMENT OF EMOTIONS
IMPACT WORDS
QUESTIONS
WORD PICTURES
STORIES
UNIVERSAL EXPERIENCES
SENSORY STIMULATING LANGUAGE
ENTRAINING EMOTIONS
SCHWARZKOPF SYNDROME
CONDITIONED INSPIRATION
PHYSIOLOGY MANAGEMENT
LEADING THROUGH VALUES

Taking Charismatic Leadership into the World

10

CREATING THE
CHARISMATIC
PRESENTATION

Being a charismatic leader requires using, on a regular basis, the elements outlined in this book. It means being persistent about inspiring others into action. It means consistently lifting their hearts, aspirations, and thus their capabilities. Much is written and spoken about organizational excellence. Yet this ability to inspire, which is at the heart of it, is seldom spoken about. *Even the best of plans requires the devoted and spirited efforts of everyone involved. Without that, success often slips away like sand between your fingers.*

To *consistently* have a charismatic effect on others, you must practice the following principles and techniques. They are flexible and can be used in an infinite variety of ways. Your goal is to reignite the spark in people, giving them the desire and excitement to move ahead. One of the greatest opportunities for us to create this level of leadership is when we give speeches. Let's take this chapter to review the steps of charismatic communication and define how to implement them to create the charismatic speech.

A SHORT COURSE IN CHARISMA

The steps of charismatic communication are a simple process to follow. Yet, when fully defined in the previous chapters, its simplicity may have been deluded in all the facts. This initial section reviews the entire process in a brief format to provide the clarity necessary to your success.

#1 Taking the High Ground

There is something you *must* do as you go through your everyday life. Charismatic leaders constantly strive to make things better. They meet all problems and opposition head-on and find solutions that work. To do that, they must maintain a view that encompasses possibility, capability, and optimism. You must do the same.

Charismatic leaders believe in the inherent greatness of the human spirit. With this comes faith that because an answer isn't apparent right now doesn't mean there won't be one tomorrow, next week, or next month. They know it's far more important to not let current problems weigh too heavily on themselves or others. They set people working immediately on solutions rather than on worrying about possible failures.

After all, it's part of the leader's job to assess potential hazards and plot the best course to follow. The burden of potential problems belongs on the shoulders of leaders. They should never transfer the weight of those problems onto others. This is the fastest way to paralyze efforts with fear.

Optimism is the thing you want to communicate to others. Optimism is a way of communicating that keeps others from losing hope in the face of opposition. It keeps minds open to the vast array of possibilities ahead. As important as this is to the process of charisma, it, too, is relatively simple. By following three basic rules you should communicate optimism with no difficulty at all.

1. Always phrase things in terms of what can be done or will be done.

2. Immediately address all problems and define them in finite terms.

3. Always provide a clear-cut course of action.

#2 Passion—the Flame of Your Soul

Charismatic leadership is not easy. It often means providing emotional energy to all those around you. *You must inspire and ignite others' best efforts every day.* Although it gets easier with time, creating the initial momentum behind a project can be exhausting. Just how exhausting depends on the task and initial level of enthusiasm of those you're leading.

That's why it's crucial that leadership and your goal are vitally important to you. Whatever your reasons may be, you must be *passionate* about your goals, the direction of your life, your job, or your leadership. Your passion is the projector that displays the importance of your objective to others.

When passion is present you become unstoppable. Passion provides you with the emotional energy needed to lead dynamically. When you are doing things vitally important to you, it's as though you are pulling strength from the heavens themselves. Others know with certainty there are urgent reasons for continuing to move ahead. They *want* to go where you are leading.

Passion creates within you a drive that's inexplicable by standard terms. It's this drive that has made the impossible possible in countless cases. When nothing is more important to you than the achievement of your goal, this kind of drive is yours. When this kind of drive is yours, you experience successes you once thought were dreams.

#3 Communicating the Emotion, Not Just the Content

You must *fully* communicate your entire message rather than just speaking words. There is no question that words are an important part of the communication process. They clarify and define human intentions and thoughts. The extraverbal aspect, however, is even more vital.

It is the extraverbal that provides emphasis, deeper meanings, and believability to the message itself. In our Western culture, we are seldom taught the importance of this level of communication. In fact, many have been led to believe just the opposite: that words solely comprise human interaction. Using only the verbal aspect of communication, however, is like going to a movie theater and hearing only the soundtrack. Without the picture, you may understand what is being said, but you don't necessarily know what is *really* going on.

If you want to have a strong effect on those around you, you must utilize the entire spectrum of the communication process. By doing so, you activate both hemispheres of your listeners' brains in a natural and harmonious fashion. You then engender confidence and feelings of honesty about your message in others. *You become your message.* This is far more powerful than having mere words speak for you.

There are two things you must do to be this effective, create this level of congruity. The first is to unleash your vocal personality. The second is to reconnect your emotions to your body, expressing emotional content through your person. Your body becomes like the speakers that broadcast the opera of your emotions out to those around you.

Your body and voice then naturally express the emotional content behind your words. Don't stifle or hold it back. Keeping emotions a closely held secret shuts people out. It makes feelings seem like guarded family secrets, things of which you are vaguely ashamed.

Allowing yourself to express the full emotional content ensures a complete message. Do not mistake this for emotional self-indulgence. Neither does it mean allowing your message to be overridden with uncontrolled feeling or hysteria. This type of display drives people away. The point of charismatic communication is to allow others in. Once up close, they can see your motivations and true intentions, believe in you, trust you.

People want to know those they follow. They want to know what their leaders are made of, what's important to them. They want their leaders to reveal themselves, for in knowledge there is trust. When leaders communicate in this open manner, others draw near, attracted by the confidence and honesty displayed before them. *Let people know who you are and they will be far more willing to follow your leadership.*

#4 Creating the Rhythm of Leadership

Charismatic leaders have magnetic personalities. The "likability factor" really refers to the uncanny ability of charismatic leaders to draw people toward them. It is one of their most striking traits.

This trait develops in a variety of ways. But it is the function of one main element: rhythm. *Rhythmic interactions are the most comfortable and enticing of all human associations.* Whenever people gather, a strong physiologic rhythm is created among them. That creates a close bond that transcends all levels of logical communication. Once strengthened and sustained for a few minutes, the bond creates the neurological link called entrainment. This is the link created by virtually every charismatic leader.

As revealed in previous chapters, entrainment can be achieved in a variety of ways. It's best, however, to initiate it by matching the natural rhythmic behavior of another or by creating the most distinct and dominant rhythm in a group of people. *Once you establish entrainment, people naturally want to listen, follow, and support you.*

Fortunately, there are a few safeguards built into this type of interaction that keep it from being abused. The main thing is that *entrainment can't be established if you are incongruent*. This means that if veering thoughts force your extraverbal behavior to conflict with your words or if you are less than truthful you will fail to entrain others. Additionally, *entrainment also eludes you if you breech the values or beliefs of those listening*.

#5 Inspiring the Greatness in Others

The hallmark of charismatic leaders is the ability to touch the hearts and minds of those they lead. *They become powerful leaders, because they harness emotions, the most powerful driver of human behavior.* They do this by using a variety of emotional-management techniques. These techniques can be used to consistently inspire the best in others. Leaders with charisma provide those they lead with the gift of powerful, positive feelings and emotions on a consistent basis.

The entire process of emotional management revolves around one main phenomenon, the ideodynamic response. The power of charisma is based on this most basic of human responses. It occurs when feelings and emotions naturally well up inside humans as they think about certain things.

The memories inside our heads are made up of a number of components. They contain at least three senses. We can sometimes see memories, hear them, and feel them. If we recall just one component, the others immediately are brought back into consciousness. For example, if you recall your favorite vacation, you can't help but have the feelings associated with those memories come tingling back.

Charismatic leaders bombard the minds of those they lead with emotional-management techniques that bring out and inspire certain feelings in them. By doing so, they get people to become motivated, move ahead, be their best. Charismatic leaders seem to bring people to action. They do this by dealing with emotions rather than with logic. They are masters of the heart *and* the head. This puts them far ahead of those who busy themselves with matters of the head, because these people lack the heart to touch others emotionally.

DESIGNING THE CHARISMATIC PRESENTATION

If you're in a leadership position, you have undoubtedly prepared numerous speeches and presentations. To create a charismatic presentation, you need add only a few additional steps to your usual procedures. Follow these steps and incorporate the techniques found throughout the book. You will be surprised at the powerful results.

#1 What major point do you want to put across?

In one way a charismatic presentation is no different from any other. *You must know your final destination before you ever start.* Most presentations we've written for others not only pivot around a central theme but include an action the presenter wants to take. It's not mandatory to include a desired action for a presentation to be charismatic. There are charismatic presentations where the sole purpose is to motivate or inspire. However, here we will consider a standard business example.

SITUATION: Your company's decline in profits can largely be attributed to outdated machinery. In your presentation you must convince your board of directors that spending reserve funds now will increase profits in the coming year. You're not at all sure that even the impressive pile of data you've accumulated will cause the board to part with a portion of the reserves. You know you must move each member at a deep level to get the action desired. You know you need more than numbers for this one. *What you say must strike their hearts as well as their minds.*

ACTION DESIRED: Purchase new, technologically advanced machinery.

#2 In what emotional state do you want to leave them?

The standard speech or presentation takes a series of points and structures them in a logical manner to support a final point or thesis. While the charismatic presentation includes the necessary information, it does not deal with structured points or ideas that follow a "logical" progression. *It uses ever-increasing emotional states culminating at the final, powerful emotional state in which you leave your audience. This final emotion or feeling should be the one that will move your audience into action.* The charismatic element of your presentation will be focused to gently guide your board members toward the desired feeling about your ideas.

FINAL EMOTION: Excitement

#3 Define the major points of your presentation.

Once again, this next step parallels standard presentation development: creating an outline prior to writing out the entire speech. Let's create the main points for our CEO.

- Introduction
- Current company losses
- There are new possibilities
- The new manufacturing technologies available
- Cost reductions competitors have enjoyed with the technology
- We've studied the possibilities for us
- Cost and savings projections
- How to introduce this new technology into our company
- What we need to do now
- Conclusion

#4 Define the emotional progression for the presentation.

In the previous step you defined the points to be made in their appropriate sequence. Now you want to define the emotional states of mind each of those sections needs to elicit. *Be sure the sequence is gradual and moves comfortably toward the final emotion.* In this case that emotion is excitement. Remember that for our purposes entrainment is an emotional state. For every presentation, you must begin with entrainment.

You should probably use the techniques heavily again just prior to infusing your audience with the final emotional state. Such a sequence could be:

- Entrainment
- Anxiety
- Interest
- Curiosity
- Intrigue
- Enthusiasm
- Heavy entrainment
- Motivation
- Excitement

#5 Develop the body of the presentation.

As you would do normally, complete your outline and create the body of your presentation. Everyone has a preferred way to do this. Some opt to initially write it out entirely, while others like heavy outlines. Whatever method you prefer, remember *you must firmly implant the presentation in your mind prior to delivery.* This will maintain congruence throughout.

#6 Integrate emotional-management techniques.

Now you have a basic presentation written out. You've listed the corresponding emotions that need to be inspired with each main point. You now need to rewrite the presentation to include emotional-management techniques.

At first this may seem somewhat cumbersome. But with practice you will be able to naturally combine steps five and six. Remember, you should attempt to apply emotional-management techniques at least three times for every emotion you wish to elicit.

It is at this stage that charismatic communication strays from standard, logical communication. You may now be tempted to lay a heavy foundation of logic to prove your point. Remember, it will be far more effective to state your point and find creative ways to emphasize those points with emotional-management techniques. For example, when stressing your competitors' use of new technology and simultaneously eliciting the emotion of intrigue, you will be better off telling stories about your competitors' overwhelming successes when facing the same kind of situation.

Remember, this is the "invisible" portion of charisma. It is that magical element that will set you apart from the rest. It will let you touch the hearts of those listening. So don't feel intimidated by replacing much of what you have written in step five with more emotionally striking language.

Additionally, your elicitation techniques don't necessarily have to logically fit in with the point you're trying to make. It might provide for smoother transitions. But even with disjointed logic, your speech won't fall apart. That's because elicitation techniques work with the unconscious rather than with the conscious mind. Don't get hung up if you can't find a story that exactly fits in. *Your primary goal is to develop a story that elicits the desired emotion.* If it directly fits in, that's just icing on the cake.

Your main tools for this phase are:

- Impact words
- Elicitation questions
- Sensory-stimulating language
- Universal experiences
- Word pictures
- Stories
- Entrainment/Congruence
- The Schwarzkopf syndrome
- Body management
- Controlling your environment

Once each of these steps have been completed you will have a more potent and inspiring presentation.

EXERCISE

To ensure a powerful presentation, once you've created the script, concentrate your practice on congruence and entrainment. With these two qualities in place, it's almost impossible to go wrong.

In the early 1980s Apple Computer was legendary for its products, meteoric growth, and incredible employee loyalty. Apple had broken all the rules of corporate America and had won. It had tenaciously battled with the giant, IBM, while others walked away.

In 1984 Apple introduced the Macintosh computer, a new and innovative product that had been the brainchild of company founder and charismatic leader Steve Jobs. Just prior to the Mac's introduction, Apple took a huge risk by releasing one of the most controversial and expensive commercials ever made. Playing off George Orwell's *1984*, the commercial showed an Orwellian world where zombielike people dressed in gray pajama suits shuffled through dimly lit corridors chained together. The next scene showed them all sitting on benches blankly staring at the omnipotent "big brother" on a large screen. Just as viewers were beginning to adjust to the strange scene unfolding before them, a young, well-built woman came running into the room clad in a bright-red Apple T-shirt and swinging a sledgehammer at the screen. As John Sculley states in his book *Odyssey*, "The screen explodes in a blinding flash of light. Then, as the camera pans the crowd, their mouths open wide as they sit mesmerized by the explosion, a voice-over says: 'On January 24th, Apple Computer will introduce Macintosh. (Pause) 1984 won't be like *1984*.'"

MAIN POINT	EMOTION NEEDED	EMOTIONAL-MANAGEMENT TECHNIQUES
Introduction	Entrainment	Vocal/Experience matching. Align with questions and directions.
Current losses	Anxiety	Universal experience
New possibility	Interest	Questions and stories
New technology in manufacturing	Curiosity	Impact words and Questions and sensory-stimulating language.
Competitors reduced $$ using the technology	Intrigue	Questions
We've studied the possibility for us	Enthusiasm	Impact words and universal experiences
What it will cost and how much it will save	Heavy entrainment	Strong congruency and alignment
How to introduce new technology	Motivation	Stories and strong congruency
What we need to do	Motivation	Universal experiences and strong congruency
Conclusion	Excitement	Story

Increasing the risk, Apple had slated the commercial to run only once, during the third quarter of the 1984 Super Bowl. Yet the chance paid off handsomely as the "1984" spot was shown on more than fifty news programs and carried on untold numbers of newspapers as being one of the most innovative approaches to advertising seen in years. The stage was set for Apple's most important product release.

On the day of the release Apple rented out a hall for employees, press, and buyers. Jobs, who had the phenomenal ability to inspire people to push far beyond their limits, knew he needed to ride the momentum already created by the "1984" spot and bring it to a crescendo with the Mac's unveiling. As recounted by John Sculley, Apple's CEO, Jobs intuitively knew how to do just that. As you read through this section from *Odyssey*, note the many techniques Jobs elegantly employs to create that "crescendo" of excitement:

> Then I introduced Steve, who walked onto a darkened stage. The real show was about to start.
>
> "It is 1958," he pronounced. "IBM passes up the chance to buy a young, fledgling company that has just invested a new technology called xerography. Two years later, Xerox is born, and IBM has been kicking itself ever since.
>
> "It is ten years later, the late sixties. Digital Equipment Corporation and others invent the minicomputer. IBM dismisses the minicomputer as too small to do serious computing and, therefore, unimportant to its business. DEC grows to become a multi-hundred-million-dollar corporation before IBM finally enters the minicomputer market.
>
> "It is now ten years later, the late seventies. In 1977, Apple, a young fledgling company on the West Coast, invents the Apple II, the first personal computer as we know it today. IBM dismisses the personal computer as

too small to do serious computing and therefore unimportant to its business.

"The early 1980s–1981. Apple II has become the world's most popular computer, and Apple has grown to a $300 million corporation, becoming the fastest-growing company in American business history. With over fifty companies vying for a share, IBM enters the personal computer market in November of 1981 with the IBM-PC.

"1983. Apple and IBM emerge as the industry's strongest competitors, each selling approximately $1 billion worth of personal computers in 1983.

". . . The shakeout is in full swing. The first major firm goes bankrupt, with others teetering on the brink. Total industry losses for 1983 overshadow even the combined profits of Apple and IBM for personal computers.

"It is now 1984. It appears IBM wants it all. Apple is perceived to be the only hope to offer IBM a run for its money. Dealers, initially welcoming IBM with open arms, now fear an IBM-dominated and controlled future. They are increasingly turning back to Apple as the only force that can ensure their future freedom."

Cheers erupt as Steve's voice grows deeper and faster.

"IBM wants it all and is aiming its guns on its last obstacle to industry control, Apple. Will Big Blue dominate the entire computer industry, the entire information age? Was George Orwell right?"

As the crowd hysterically shouted a chorus of "No's," the "1984" commercial hit the huge screen behind Steve. It was a brilliant bit of theatrics, a prelude to his official introduction of the Macintosh. Until then, there had only been two milestone products in personal computers—the Apple II and the IBM-PC. Macintosh was meant to be the third milestone.

Steve walked over to a bag, unzipped it, and took the computer out, just as theatrically as he had done many months earlier when he was trying to lure a Pepsi-Cola president to the company.

As he turned on the Mac, the theme of the movie *Chariots of Fire* blasted from the auditorium's speakers . . .

. . . The audience roared its approval. The first five rows of the auditorium were filled with members of the Macintosh team—all dressed in Mac T-shirts—who led the explosion. No one could help getting carried away by the hysteria. Not the shareholders nor the media. Steve, a knowing smile on his face, nodded his head back and forth. He knew he had them in the palm of his hand. For a minute, he had created more than "an insanely great" product. He had created a church . . .

. . . Never before in my life had I felt such emotional exhilaration.

Adhere to the principles of charismatic communication and virtually anything can be turned into a celebration of monumental proportions.

In Short

1. Creating a charismatic presentation is just as straightforward as putting together any other type of presentation. The first step consists of defining the major points you want to put across and knowing precisely what action you want out of your audience.

2. What emotional state of mind do you want to leave your audience in? Remember, it must coincide with the ultimate actions you want created.

3. Define the major points of your presentation.

4. Define the emotional progression for the presentation. This progression can coincide with the major points of the presentation or be completely independent.

5. Develop the body of the presentation. This is primarily the time when you collect the logical information for the presentation.

6. Integrate emotional management techniques. We have supplied ten techniques that can be used individually, together, and in any combination. You're only restricted by your creativity.

11

MAKING YOUR IMPACT ON THE WORLD

In the previous pages, we broke charismatic communication down to its components and presented them in rather technical fashion. This was necessary to explain them in the way your mind accepts and processes the written word. Now, *it's time to begin working with the concept*. The basics you have learned between the pages of this book will come alive in your life. You will make them uniquely yours.

Technical information becomes in practice something very different. The goal of charismatic communication is far different from that of logical interactions based on the transfer of information. *As a charismatic leader your primary purpose is to inspire the best in others*. All other considerations are secondary.

To truly inspire requires this most graceful form of communication. It's not unlike learning ballet. You must understand the structure and form of the dance and begin practicing individual steps. But, once learned, the dance becomes a graceful expression of precise elegance. Charismatic communication is an art form, neither static nor abrasive. Rather, it's as fluid and smooth as running water, swaying with the needs, desires, and aspirations of people.

In this chapter, you will review skills learned in this book and additional ways to apply them to your everyday life. These are really your starting point. You will continue to integrate and re-create charismatic communication that is unique to you and the goals for your life.

DEVELOPING THE HIGH-PERFORMANCE WORK PLACE

As employers, managers, leaders we have all seen the best-laid plans fall apart and never reach their intended goals. Too many people make the most carefully forecasted calculations that leave one critical element to the wind. This is the consistent, day-to-day performance of those who execute those plans.

Although people normally wish to do their best, they are frequently ambushed by a variety of unwanted intruders into the work place. These intruders come clinging to the backs of those responsible for making things work. The interlopers have names. They include Anxiety, Depression, Worthlessness, Guilt, and Loneliness. We hire beaming faces and enthusiastic attitudes. But, sooner or later, everyone comes to work with a stowaway or two. These thugs sap productivity and effectiveness, turning champions into lightweight contenders not quite up to the challenge.

The Charisma Factor has a natural application in the work place. The job of the charismatic leader is to eliminate unwanted intruders. They must be replaced with strong, resourceful, and enduring positive emotions. With these emotions in your corner, you are able to turn your team into a work force to rival any. When training, education, and razor-honed planning aren't enough, infuse the absolute best in people. It's time to gear up their emotional energy, letting it go to work for them and for you.

Under the guidance of charismatic leaders, many employees find work their sanctuary from the world. They wake up looking forward to the workday. They are exuberant about what they do. This is because an environment has been created that pulls out the best in them. They like to be where they feel secure, innovative, useful, and successful.

Look around such a work place and you will find at least one charismatic leader. Charisma is the "magic" component that bridges the gap between management and leadership. It gives you the tools to inspire the best in people and get them to want to follow your leadership. This section provides you with a blueprint to create organizational excellence, to put into place that final element of leadership strategy.

Leaders have a responsibility to create an environment that promotes the achievement of their goals. This obviously includes the appropriate rules, regulations, organizational structure, and other management functions necessary in any good company. But it also includes an ingredient too often overlooked in modern business practices. *Do you have an environment that creates and sustains positive emotional states in your employees?* If you don't, you have problems. *This is the only type of environment that will allow your employees to naturally and consistently respond in ways that keep everything moving in the intended direction.*

Consider any organization that has accomplished great things in short periods. There is one thing of which you can be sure. There were leaders who created an environment that naturally elicited and sustained the most powerful and positive emotions in their employees. Steven Jobs, a co-founder of Apple Computer, obviously understood the importance of this principle.

> ... he went to great lengths to build and sustain the team that produced the company's potent Macintosh. Jobs had to maneuver himself into position as head of the development team over objections from some other company executives. Once there, he went to consider-

able lengths to keep the creative current flowing. He set his team apart from the rest of the company, at one point flying a pirate flag over its building to signify their determination to blow a rival team out of the water; he staged frequent parties, sushi dinners, and seaside retreats; he presented medals, and sometimes stock options in thin gray envelopes to star performers; he had the development team's name embossed, "for posterity," on the inside of the mold for the machine's case; he bullied, threatened, and adopted slogans like "The journey is the reward"; he surrounded the entire project with his conviction that "the Macintosh is the future of Apple Computer." (Garfield, 1986)

Notice the reference to keeping the "creative current flowing." Jobs created an environment that would spawn and sustain a specific emotional state, one that would keep his team directed toward a specific outcome. The "creative current," translated into The Charisma Factor lexicon, would be the emotional state. This was probably a mixture of creativity, motivation, excitement, and dedication that Jobs knew was necessary for success.

Getting superior leadership results isn't due to being in some magic time or place. It is a very distinct process. The following steps provide that process. They have been used by thousands of successful leaders for centuries. The only difference is that in the past, if you weren't lucky enough to stumble across the right steps, true charismatic leadership remained a mystery.

Take each of the following steps in the order in which they appear. Move on to the next only when you feel you have mastered each preceding one within your organization. The Charisma Factor is a methodical and straightforward process. *Remain focused.* As you're testing and experimenting it could take a few weeks to fully implement your first program. With practice, once you have a well-defined goal, you can often do the rest within a day!

Preparing for Dynamic Leadership

Despite its powerful applications, *charismatic leadership does not eliminate the need for thorough preparation. Success in any complex endeavor requires a well-thought-out and well-executed plan.* Without this you are on a one-way trip to failure no matter how charismatic you may be. Therefore, your first task is to have a clearly defined direction, an ultimate goal. It should be so firmly implanted in your mind that you know how it will look, sound, feel, and taste once completed. You must be intimately associated with every detail.

Sure of each basic step in your plan, you must also know who among your staff will make those steps. Your goal is vital. But it alone is not sufficient. *You must have mental command of the entire implementation process and the role of each player.* Get a solid grasp of all variables.

Additionally, *every charismatic leader knows the kind of emotional assistance each employee requires to perform at his or her optimum.* Some need strong motivation and constant inspiration. Others need confidence, while still others must be calmed and soothed. Paying attention to these may not be part of your normal operating procedure. But *to create sustained excellence you must be sensitive to others' normal emotional states of mind.* Then you can decide if or how they require change.

Remember how much work charismatic leadership is. *Be certain the project is one about which you are passionate.* This is the energizer that will move you toward great action. Remember: *by sheer passionate energy people have achieved unbelievable things time and time again.* Before you ever consider charismatically leading your employees, be sure you have enough passion for the project. This will drive your best efforts as well as infuse drive in those around you. If you are truly passionate about your direction, chances are it's important enough to enlist the help of others.

EXERCISE

Notice the level of motivation in each of your immediate employees. Rate them on a continuum from passionately committed to their job down to the pessimistic energy drainers. This will let you know whom you can count on to give their best efforts and who will initially require a good deal of your time.

The ways most great charismatic leaders demonstrate their passionate commitment toward a project is to constantly communicate direction with enthusiasm. Whenever possible (without becoming overbearing and while maintaining entrainment) bring up the benefits and applications of your direction. Another powerful method of demonstrating passionate commitment is to use elicitation techniques, such as impact words. *You can intertwine your team members' enthusiasm with your own by eliciting their most powerful emotions.* Carefully structure your every approach toward them. Inspire the passion in them. They, too, will take on the cause, making it their own.

Remember: You must be sure you can talk about your leadership congruently. Congruence is believability. *If you want to inspire others to their finest efforts, you must show superior dedication.* You lead by example. You *must* personify the direction. If you want others to take this project and direction to heart, it must be firmly implanted in your's first. You must be out in front. Charismatic leaders don't lead from behind; they show others the way.

Pulling Your Team Together

Before even proposing your project, pull your team together. *You need to develop the foundation for leadership prior to enlisting their efforts.* You must develop a level of entrainment with each person on the team and be comfortable with leading the team. In addition, you need to create a harmonious work environment where everyone works in total sync and naturally follows your lead. This lays the groundwork for your future leadership success.

All great charismatic leaders have had the ability to make those around them feel comfortable and connected. They entrain with others, even without knowing it. They take the time to find out what their employees are really like. They go out of their way to make sure others are comfortable. This doesn't necessarily mean they create deep, abiding friendship—just entrainment. They sync with their employees to be sure they're comfortable. Others feel part of the team, that they're important.

We've detailed a variety of techniques for matching and syncing with others to gain acceptance. *It's your responsibility to do whatever it takes within ethical boundaries to develop a bond with those on your team.* At the same time you need to develop complete comfort in leading each individual. You must be sure you have the ability to lead each one before getting the project underway. This can best be done by syncing and leading each individual on your staff several times. Be sure you're confident with your syncing and leading skills as outlined in previous chapters.

Once entrainment has been built a few times individually, it's time to align the team. Make them a singularly functioning unit under your leadership. It will take some creativity on your part to come up with the appropriate methods for your staff so don't limit yourself to just the ideas in this book. Group alignment means getting them all to do something together in an identical manner. Remember, many "Team Building" exercises don't work well because they demonstrate differences rather than similarities, the essence of alignment. Brainstorming sessions fall into this category. Since most people perceive the world somewhat differently, brainstorming sessions focus on differences. This doesn't mean they aren't great for an appropriate purpose. But they are not effective for *aligning* the team.

As a leader, you must align your teams periodically to reinforce not only the "team" but your leadership of it. There are literally thousands of ways to do this. Getting the team to exercise together is great—especially something aerobic. Get out and walk together as you discuss ideas. "Field trips" are great. If you're working on a construction project, get the team out to the site. Visit a vendor. Attend a trade show. What's important is keeping people together doing the same things. It needn't be anything elaborate, as long as they're aligned as a team. Don't forget about music playing in the background. Consider having the team develop a slogan or create a flag. Make it fun. *Charisma can be fun when you let it.* It feels good to be part of a group where everyone is achieving his or her best. If you do it right, soon everyone will want to be on your team.

The Kick-Off

Once your plan is thoroughly laid out it's time to kick off the project. This is often important to a charismatic leader's ultimate success. A strong kick-off lays the groundwork. It sets the emotional tone of the project. Your job is to define the appropriate overall emotional tone and work it into the presentation. Some people will require enthusiasm, others perseverance, while still others must have confidence. All can be provided with emotional-management techniques.

A great kick-off often takes the form of a strong charismatic presentation. It should encompass the elements of your project and infuse a strong and motivating set of emotions in your team. It should be the inspirational hallmark of the project and the foundation of your long-term charismatic leadership. Plan it well. *The stronger the kick-off, the easier your following day-to-day job will be.*

Maintaining the Environment

When you've heard an effective motivational speaker, you have probably felt outstanding. The emotions infused into you during the presentation kept you feeling that way for a period of time—usually a week or two. After awhile the effect dissipates. Charismatic leadership also wears off. Therefore, *people require a periodic infusion of positive emotions.* If you want to keep people at their best and maintain a strong working environment, you must continue to inspire their hearts.

This requires you to be sensitive to each team member's emotional state of mind. In addition to natural emotional fluctuations, people experience setbacks, minor failures, difficulties from outside the work place. These all affect performance. Your job is to be aware when this happens so you can pull them back into a resourceful state of mind. Caution should be used. There's a fine line between being charismatic and being annoying. You can be overzealous. It is unrealistic to think you can maintain a peak state in everyone all the time. There are natural emotional fluctuations throughout the day. These shouldn't be interfered with. It's when you notice people continuing to slip over a period of several days that you step in.

Maintaining a productive environment can be done in an infinite number of ways. Oftentimes, it takes nothing more than putting a smile on the face of your employees a few times a day. Other times you may prefer to get together with them one at a time. Once again, it doesn't matter so much *what* you do as long as you are getting the response you want.

One of the easiest phenomena that leaders can take advantage of to maintain high performance is the Hawthorne Effect. This discovery was made years ago at the Western Electric Company in Chicago, where researchers were experimenting with the effects of working conditions on different employee groups. They dealt with a variety of conditions such as lighting, work hours, and incentive pay. Yet, regardless what they did, whether they made working conditions better or worse, productivity went up. Although initially baffled, researchers finally determined that it wasn't the environmental factors that created productivity boosts but the attention paid them by management and researchers alike. Your simple undivided attention to a person or work unit can bring about increases of many kinds. You should, at the least, schedule in time to contact each person or group whose performance is vital to your company's success.

Steve Jobs developed a wonderful blue print for the constant types of efforts which must be employed to maintain high levels of excellence. He created theme parties. Slogans were composed, flags flown, awards given. All were meant to maintain a certain emotional environment for his employees. Even Sam Walton, the founder of Wal-Mart stores, belived in constantly doing virtually anything necessary to capture the attention and excitement of his employees. He would routinely turn standard meetings into celebrations which looked more like revivals rather than business gatherings. In an interview Walton stated that "I have a cheer I lead whenever I visit a store. For those of you who don't know, it goes like this:

Give me a W!
Give me an A!
Give me an L!
Give me a Squiggly!
(Here, everybody sort of does the twist).
Give me an M!
Give me an A!
Give me an R!
Give me a T!
What's that spell?
Wal-Mart!
What's that spell?
Wal-Mart!
Who's No. 1?
THE CUSTOMER

"And if I'm leading the cheer, you'd better believe we do it loud. My feeling is that just because we work so hard, we don't have to go around with long faces all the time, taking ourselves seriously, pretending we're lost in thought over weighty problems" (Walton, 1992). Given everything we've reviewed thus far in THE CHARISMA FACTOR, what kind of leader would you classify the legendary Sam Walton?

"Charismatic Communication is more than a mere leadership technique, it's a gift you give to those you work with."

As a leader your job is more than simple goal development and profit enhancement. It's to help people grow, feel vital and worthy, and to walk away with a deep knowledge that they have accomplished something worthwhile. Then and only then is a leader really a leader. They haven't just used the talents of their people for their own or the organization's good. They have given them each a personal sense of worth and value, they have let them grow. They have given back to them in a profound way.

EXERCISE

During your project planning phase make a list of events, ideas, and strategies that you can implement on a moment's notice to reinvigorate the emotional energy of your team. Being prepared will give you the ability to react to any eventuality on a moment's notice.

Some could be:
  Parties
  Gifts
  Celebrations
  Recognition
  Picnics
  Slogans
  Theme events

Bringing Them Back on Track

From time to time, even the best people will have bad days. On these days they bring their personal lives and the burdens of the world into work with them. The high-performance team is well directed and remains in powerful, resourceful emotional states. But it is virtually impossible for even a charismatic leader to keep everyone there daily. It is imperative, however, that none of the team members walks around in a negative or unresourceful state for a prolonged period of time. If you notice one of your team members in such a condition, bring them back up and do it in a hurry. If a team member had cholera, would you let him or her walk around infecting the rest of the team, hoping everyone would feel better soon? Negative states of mind are no less threatening or contagious. There's a way to deal with this disease. *Diffuse negative emotions.*

As you know, for human beings to remain in any emotional state, they must internally focus on something. When people come to work in a bad mood and remain there, it's because they're constantly thinking about or focusing upon whatever is making them feel that way. For instance, some people will have a fight with their spouse before work and just keep replaying the incident. They remain upset. It's like a record needle that's stuck and playing the same thing over and over. As you've learned, diffusions quickly change people's thoughts. You can do it any number of ways: surprise, confusion, interest, and so forth, as long as the diffusion does something out of the ordinary. *Diffusions force people to think of other things. And when thoughts change so do emotions.*

Also remember, it's important not to attempt to jump people from one extreme to another. You can't take someone from anger to happiness in one step. No matter how entrained we may be, we will probably fail. The gap between emotions is too wide. People need to be gradually moved from one emotional state to the next. You can move them from anger to upset, to annoyed, to calm, to amusement, to laughter, to happiness. It's effective to gently move people along a chain of emotions by focusing their thoughts.

Diffusions speed up this process. If you interrupt internal thoughts, people can't remain in the state they were in.

It's impossible. All you have to do is wrest their thoughts away from the source of the negative state for a few minutes. Being unable to think about whatever fed the negativity is like cutting off the electricity to an electrically powered motor. It dies. The steps to help someone get away from his or her current way of thinking could be:

> Establish entrainment
>
> Defuse thoughts
>
> Redirect him or her by giving something different to concentrate on

You could, for example, use confusion since it's an especially powerful state. Remember, human beings naturally want to understand their environment. When people become confused their minds instantly begin searching through memories for meaning to what is happening. During this time, we can get them to think about positive ideas, leading them on the path of beneficial emotions.

An example would be a meeting between Tom, a department manager, and Lou, one of his best employees.

TOM:	Well, I think I've seen you looking a little better in days past.
LOU:	(Speaking in a growl) Sorry, Tom, this just isn't a day for talking. My mind's on other things.
TOM:	(Matching Lou's posture and syncing with his vocal tempo) I can see that, and that's okay. We're all entitled.
LOU:	If you don't mind, I'll just see you later at the meeting, Tom.
TOM:	(Knowing that trying to talk with Lou while he's in this state would be nonproductive, Tom begins to defuse his thinking using confusion techniques) Sure.

Oh, by the way, would you bring together the agenda for the meeting necessary for coupling to the extent we need till yesterday.

LOU: (Looking at Tom, puzzled) What are you talking about?

TOM: (Continuing to match and sync with Lou and remaining *totally congruent* as he speaks) You remember this is the same issue brought up during last week's future agenda happening a month from now. I'd just like you, when convenient, to complete the statements on an ongoing way from that older subject to one better suited for us here. In that time from now you will have the opportunity for betterment of the organization. (Tom places one hand on Lou's shoulder and points rather vaguely across the room.) That's why over there will be a better place to organize that function for then. (Tom, noticing a blank look on Lou's face—a good indication of total confusion—begins to lead him to a more resourceful emotional state.) Hey, do you remember the picnic last month? (Tom emphasizes a time he knows Lou was in a great emotional state, thus eliciting the memory of the time.) Remember when Tony was talking about . . . well, in between the times you two were laughing. By the way, what was it that was so funny? I mean, I've never seen you laughing so hard. (Lou starts to get a small smile on his face.) Everytime I've seen Tony since then he always seems to be chuckling.

LOU: (Smiling) Oh, we were just goofing around. You know Tony. You can't get that guy to give a straight answer to anything. I was trying to have at least one serious conversation with him during the picnic, and he shot that all to hell.

TOM: (The change in Lou's thoughts and the better emotional state he's in lets Tom knows he's helping.) Well, tell you what. The meeting is not too far off—why don't you walk with me there, and I'll take care of the rest of the project (taking the walk to change Lou's physiology).

LOU: (Still smiling) Sure! By the way, I'm sorry but I don't remember that agenda thing.

TOM: Oh, that's okay. On second thought, I'll just take care of it.

THE CHARISMATIC SALES STRATEGY

Most of the best sales professionals have charisma. They don't simply go out and attempt to sell the benefits of a product. They embody them and use them to engage the enthusiasm of their prospects. A powerful interaction occurs each time they make a call. They get people to *want* to buy the product rather than pressuring the sale. Here's an application of how it can work for you.

Scenario: After the research for *The Charisma Factor* was completed, there came the unique task of selling a concept previously considered impossible: that of providing charismatic traits to anyone. Selling training programs was no different from selling any other product or service. It could most effectively be done using charismatic communication. If customers were in the appropriate emotional state of mind when being shown the benefits of the program, they would want to purchase the training. There would be no need to apply any of the standard sales techniques or go through the traditional closing routines. People would just ask for it.

The following application is a condensed version of how the program was sold to a variety of companies. Remember, developing a sales script is really no different from doing so for any other application. You follow the steps. Once entrainment has been developed, each emotional-management technique should be delivered passionately and congruently. Your entire being should communicate the emotional state you're trying to elicit.

RESULT DESIRED: Schedule a training
TARGET STATE: Want or desire
STATE SEQUENCE:

Sequence	Emotional Management
Entrainment	Syncing
Curiosity	Questions
Interest	Word pictures
Fascination	Universal experience and questions
Excitement	Entraining emotions
Want	Universal experience

In any sales encounter entrainment is one of the most vital issues. Before you move into your presentation be sure it is already well in place. When people sit down for a sales meeting they will usually chitchat for a while. This is meant to create a comfortable atmosphere. It is our natural attempt to develop entrainment, even when we're unaware of it.

There is a critical error many salespeople make. It is one you want to avoid. Once you move into your presentation, do not break the entrainment you have developed. Too often the transition from entrainment development to presentation results in the salesperson changing his or her vocal quality (tone and tempo especially), posture, and gestures.

This abrupt transition ruins entrainment. It communicates to the client that the "personal" conversation is over. Now it's time to put up the barriers because the sales pitch is about to start. On the other hand, a smooth transition maintains entrainment while your presentation progresses. We'll move into this scenario with the assumption that entrainment, thus a comfortable personal relationship, has already been established.

CONDENSED SCRIPT

CLIENT: So, what's this work I've been hearing so much about? Something about being able to have charisma, isn't it?

SALESPRO: (Working toward the state of curiosity) Yes. And, since you've already seen the information pack, you know how all this started in the first place. (The client's mind begins searching for the story he read.) You know, when we started the study we couldn't believe how *intensely curious* we became in just the first few days. I mean, it was like being a little kid again on the day before Christmas, just dying to know what those presents are. (Universal experience) As a matter of fact, we even had difficulty sleeping through much of the project in anticipation of the results. (Universal experience)

(Working toward the state of interest) So, once we'd compiled what seemed like a mountain of data, we began sifting through it to see if we could find that common thread linking all those charismatic leaders together. I mean, what did these people do that made them so great? (Question matches the question of interest in the client's mind.) In time, we began to catch glints of that needle in the haystack. (Word picture) And, do you know precisely what charisma turned out to be . . . I mean, the real foundational element of charismatic leadership? (Question)

(Working toward fascination) Can you remember a time when you listened to a charismatic leader or speaker? Maybe a speech by John Kennedy or Ronald Reagan. One of those people who can really make you feel inspired? Or in their cases, just made you feel good about the country. Can you remember at least one time? (A series of universal experiences and questions interwoven. Client nods head yes, while a slight smile comes over his face.) As you look back over that time and hear the speech, if you really think about it, they probably didn't even say anything of great importance. But in another way they did. Because charismatic communication doesn't target the giving of information, but of emotions.

Think about it. Maybe *what* they said wasn't of really great importance, but *how they made you feel* was. You felt good. That memory you have in your mind now, did you feel inspired, proud, or *fascinated*? That is the crux of charisma right there. It's the ability to manage the emotions of others. To be able to truly touch hearts and minds. And you know how important that is, because we are all emotionally driven creatures. If you provide the necessary emotions, people will naturally want to do virtually anything ethical that you ask.

But I'll tell you what I think is the most important thing about this training. It's that it takes what has been a natural gift possessed by a few great leaders and breaks it down into simple techniques *anyone can learn*. In truth, *everyone* has charisma within them. The only problem in the past has been knowing what to do to release it. How can we have a charismatic impact on others? A perfect example is Oliver North. After the better part of a year of being battered by the press, he turned the thoughts of an entire nation in just a few hours of testimony. In just days, there were calls of Ollie for President. (Universal experience) (Excitement) *The power of personal charisma is stunning*.

(Developing want or desire) Each of us can only imagine the kinds of things *we would* be able to get done if we possessed this information. When you can manage the emotions of those around you, *you will* have the ability to powerfully control your environment. We've all dreamt of having a road map that could guide us to virtually any of our goals. What we have here is the most advanced and complete map known today. We both know that *every leader wants* to have the ability to lead others through any endeavor. And charisma has been one of the most *sought after and desired* traits known. People in all walks of life *want it* and will *use it right away*.

TURNING POLITICAL MESSES INTO POLITICAL SUCCESSES

You do not have to limit the techniques in this book to be one-on-one interactions or basic speeches or presentations. The ability to manage the emotions of groups of people can be used in a variety of ways. In this section, we review the use of these techniques, using a more creative application. Notice as the strategy unfolds that this could have been a difficult political situation. It was handled by essentially ignoring "facts." The entire situation was controlled so we could address the true issues.

Scenario

A midsized city was embroiled in a political battle between the city's senior community and its local government. The senior citizens, who made up a powerful voting block, were consistently finding more and more fault with the city council they had voted into power. In fact, they felt the council had not fulfilled campaign promises to them. They felt betrayed.

The local newspapers didn't help. They constantly ran articles on a variety of senior issues *not* being handled by the government. Cries for recall were beginning to be heard. Government officials became frantic as their endless meetings with senior representatives and subsequent new policies failed to curb the problem.

An investigation of the issue showed that most of the problems evolved from residents living in mobile home parks. Coincidentally, they were predominantly senior citizens and very vocal about local issues. Interviews with a number of seniors made it obvious that the main problem was actually simple. Most seniors felt they were being overlooked by their city government. Things just weren't as they were when this was a smaller city. Nobody *cared* about anybody else.

In their eyes the worst offender was local government. It was now a large bureaucratic entity. Despite all the rhetoric, it was a government that didn't really care about its citizens. If you think about it, these were people who lived during a time when customer service meant personal service. In their time when they pulled into a gas station five attendants came rushing to their car; when the people you dealt with called you by name and talked to you face-to-face, not through a mass-produced letter.

Personal service was the *real* reason they voted the city council into office in the first place. What they got was a bureaucracy that didn't respond. Everything stayed the same. They still felt the chill of policies and programs that they felt were designed to keep them out of the way and quiet. That's what these people told us over and over. Yet, interestingly, the city council had completed or was vigorously working on completing *every* campaign promise they had made to the senior community.

Armed with this information, we looked for the approach that would communicate a different message to this special group. Surprisingly, the opportunity came to us. A week into this project, a city building inspector went through mobile-home parks and cited *more than 90 percent* of the coaches with a variety of building-code violations. The violation form left hanging on each door knob contained a standard statement of violation and a building-code violation number. It also said something like: "Failure to fully comply with rectification of said violation within 30 days will result in billing by the city for said work or eviction from the premises."

The entire senior community was enraged. Their elected officials had betrayed them once again. Now people who had worked hard all their lives and lived by the rules had been given what was perceived as eviction notices even though they hadn't even known something was wrong with their homes. The press had a field day.

As bad as it was, the situation offered an opportunity to put things right. We met with city officials to find out how the city could help these citizens. First, the officials could explain exactly what each violation was. They could then provide basic plans for fixing the problems in each home. Additionally, they had full listings of contractors, plumbers, and builders who could do the work. And, finally, there were a number of financial assistance plans that could entirely pay for the projects. That sounded as if it would be really good news for the seniors. Of course, normal procedure would be for the city to mail out the information in yet another cold letter filled with information and bureaucratic jargon. The good intentions would get lost in cold type.

Instead, we called a "town meeting" at a mobile-home park for everyone who had been cited. Some seniors we had come to know well were asked to bring snacks. We invited the press as well as the rest of the senior community to join us. We wanted to create an environment where a positive relationship between city officials and the senior community could develop. We wanted, for the first time, to create that personal relationship the seniors wanted.

We had a number of advantages. First, we knew what the seniors really wanted: a more personal local government. Second, we knew we would have time to diffuse their anger. Because they didn't know specifically what was wrong with their property, they had to listen to us before they could go on the offensive. We also knew they were decent and responsible people who wanted safe homes and wanted to abide by the rules. Finally, the city was prepared for the first time to provide more personal service.

The hall was filled to capacity. Hundreds of citizens mingled with press and community leaders. We had previously prepared personal packets for each cited home-owner. It contained detailed information on the work that needed to be done and what services were available through the city. We made sure government representatives attending were either well liked in the senior community or unknown to them. Seniors had expressed negative feelings about some. They were asked not to attend. We didn't want anyone there whose presence could incite problems.

The building department director opened with a speech outlining the entire program. It had been prepared, however, to create a harmonious environment with entrainment techniques. Once the presentation was completed, city employees personally passed out the information packets to each cited citizen. They chatted and then scheduled a date at their convenience when a building inspector could come to their home. They were told they would have all the time they needed to work out the problem and arrange for financial aid.

The effect of this small extra touch was astounding. For the first time, the seniors felt the city was responding to their needs. They finally had won a victory. The most important sign for us was that at the close of the meeting no one left. More snacks and coffee were brought in. The seniors and city employees stayed together talking and getting to know one another. There were the beginnings of sound, personal relationships. The press carried nothing but positive stories about the meeting. A political issue that was on its way to a recall election ended up creating even stronger support for the city council.

Too many company and organization issues are dealt with at a logical and standard business level. The problems get larger and more distant from human feeling. Yet, often the biggest problems can be solved with the smallest efforts. It's just that they must be the right efforts. All those citizens wanted was something their government was more than capable of giving them. Just by a simple change in "standard operating procedure" citizens began to feel government really belonged to them. Their response was to openly support and back their official's efforts. How many huge problems exist simply because we deal with them on a cold, logical level rather than give people what they emotionally need?

CONCLUSION

> Without the hero, the community lacks a crucial dimension, for the hero is typically the soul of the community. Heroes are necessary in order to enable the citizens to find their own ideals, courage, and the wisdom in the society."
>
> Rollo May
> "The Cry for Myth"

Not all heroes are leaders, but all leaders must be heroes to those they would guide. Today, we hear the plea for someone to come forth with a light. We have not yet measured the distance from who we are to who it is within us to be. We guess at just how far we have to go and watch our horizon with fearful eyes. If only, we think, there were someone who knew the way.

There are many paths through the dark woods, but few are brave enough to walk them. Fewer still are those who believe so deeply in their own vision and the splendor of the human soul that they risk saying, "Follow me" as they begin the journey.

And yet, for those few, life is not a way station where they find comfort in sameness. It's a journey. Along the way, they are blessed with the opportunity to fully enjoy the struggles and the triumphs it offers.

Those of you who lead from the heart are fueled by their passion. This enables you not only to realize your own dreams but to help others find theirs. That is when you forever leave the stricture of limits and begin to dwell in the realm of possibility. Once there, you find that discovery is the prize, and becoming who you are is the everyday joy. Godspeed.

BIBLIOGRAPHY

Beckwith, Charlie, and Donald Knox. *Delta Force*. New York: Harcourt Brace Jovanovich, 1983.

Brown, Peter. *The Hypnotic Brain*. New Haven: Yale University Press, 1991.

Erickson, Milton H., Ernest L. Rossi, and Sheila I. Rossi. *Hypnotic Realities*. New York: Irvington Publishers, 1976.

Fehrenbacher, Don, ed. *Lincoln: Selected Speeches and Writings*. New York: Vintage Books, 1992.

Garfield, Charles. *Peak Performers*. New York: Avon Books, 1986.

Glass, Lillian. *Talk To Win*. New York: The Putnam Publishing Group, 1987.

Hall, Edward T. *Beyond Culture*. New York: DoubleDay, 1976.

Hall, Edward T. *The Dance Of Life*. New York: DoubleDay, 1983.

Hall, Edward T. *The Silent Language*. New York: DoubleDay, 1959.

Hillkirk, John, and Gary Jocobson. *Grit, Guts & Genius*. Boston: Houghton Mifflin Company, 1990.

Lakoff, George, and Mark Johnson. *Metaphors We Live By*. Chicago: University Of Chicago Press, 1980.

May, Rollo. *The Cry For Myth*. New York: W.W. Norton & Company, 1991.

McCrone, John. *The Ape That Spoke*. New York: William Morrow & Company, Inc, 1991.

Mehrabian, Albert, and S.R. Ferris. *Inference of Attitudes from Nonverbal Communication in Two Channels*. Journal of Consulting Psychology 31, 1967.

Ravitch, Diane, ed. *The American Reader*. New York: HarperCollins, 1990.

Reagan, Ronald. *Speaking My Mind*. New York: Simon & Schuster, 1989.

Restak, Richard. *The Brain Has A Mind Of It's Own*. New York: Harmony Books, 1991.

Sacks, Oliver. *Awakenings*. New York: HarperCollins Publishers, 1973.

Sacks, Oliver. *The Man Who Mistook His Wife For A Hat*. New York: HarperPerennial, 1970.

Scheflen, A.E. *Interactional Rhythms*. New York: Human Sciences Press, 1982.

Sculley, John. *Odyssey*. New York: Harper & Row, 1987.

Seligman, Martin. *Learned Optimism*. New York: Pocket Books, 1990.

Shafritz, Jay M., ed. *Words On War*. New York: Prentice Hall, 1990.

Smalley, Gary., and John Trent. *The Language Of Love*. Pomona: Focus On The Family Books, 1988.

Sorensen, Theodore C., ed. *"Let The Word Go Forth"*. New York: Dell Publishing, 1988.

Thomas, David R. *Dave's Way*. New York: G.P. Putman's Sons, 1991.

Transcripts were provided by Federal News Service, 620 National Press Building, Washington, D.C. 20045.

Walton, Sam. *Made In America*. New York: DoubleDay, 1992.

The Testimony Of Lieutenant Colonel Oliver North. *Taking The Stand*. New York: Pocket Books, 1987.

INDEX